I0706405

THE SCOURGE OF
RUSSIAN DISINFORMATION

HEARING

BEFORE THE

COMMISSION ON SECURITY AND COOPERATION IN EUROPE

ONE HUNDRED FIFTEENTH CONGRESS

FIRST SESSION

SEPTEMBER 14, 2017

Printed for the use of the
Commission on Security and Cooperation in Europe

[CSCE 115–1–5]

Available via www.csce.gov

U.S. GOVERNMENT PUBLISHING OFFICE

26–880 PDF   WASHINGTON : 2017

For sale by the Superintendent of Documents, U.S. Government Publishing Office
Internet: bookstore.gpo.gov   Phone: toll free (866) 512–1800; DC area (202) 512–1800
Fax: (202) 512–2104   Mail: Stop IDCC, Washington, DC 20402–0001

COMMISSION ON SECURITY AND COOPERATION IN EUROPE

LEGISLATIVE BRANCH COMMISSIONERS

HOUSE

CHRISTOPHER H. SMITH, New Jersey,
Co-Chairman
ALCEE L. HASTINGS, Florida
ROBERT B. ADERHOLT, Alabama
MICHAEL C. BURGESS, Texas
STEVE COHEN, Tennessee
RICHARD HUDSON, North Carolina
RANDY HULTGREN, Illinois
SHIELA JACKSON LEE, Texas
GWEN MOORE, Wisconsin

SENATE

ROGER F. WICKER, Mississippi,
Chairman
BENJAMIN L. CARDIN, Maryland
JOHN BOOZMAN, Arkansas
CORY GARDNER, Colorado
MARCO RUBIO, Florida
JEANNE SHAHEEN, New Hampshire
THOM TILLIS, North Carolina
TOM UDALL, New Mexico
SHELDON WHITEHOUSE, Rhode Island

EXECUTIVE BRANCH COMMISSIONERS

Vacant, Department of State
Vacant, Department of Commerce
Vacant, Department of Defense

[II]

THE SCOURGE OF RUSSIAN DISINFORMATION

COMMISSIONERS

WITNESSES

APPENDICES

THE SCOURGE OF
RUSSIAN DISINFORMATION

September 14, 2017

Commission on Security and Cooperation in Europe

Washington, DC

The hearing was held at 9:34 a.m. in Room 562, Dirksen Senate Office Building, Washington, DC, Hon. Cory Gardner, Commissioner, Commission on Security and Cooperation in Europe, presiding.

Commissioners present: Hon. Cory Gardner, Commissioner, Commission on Security and Cooperation in Europe; Hon. Christopher Smith, Co-Chairman, Commission on Security and Cooperation in Europe; Hon. Benjamin L. Cardin, Ranking Member, Commission on Security and Cooperation in Europe; Hon. Gwen Moore, Commissioner, Commission on Security and Cooperation in Europe; Hon. Jeanne Shaheen, Commissioner, Commission on Security and Cooperation in Europe; and Hon. Sheldon Whitehouse, Commissioner, Commission on Security and Cooperation in Europe.

Witnesses present: John F. Lansing, Chief Executive Officer and Director, Broadcasting Board of Governors (BBG); Molly K. McKew, CEO, Fianna Strategies; and Melissa Hooper, Director of Human Rights and Civil Society Programs, Human Rights First.

HON. CORY GARDNER, COMMISSIONER, COMMISSION ON SECURITY AND COOPERATION IN EUROPE

Mr. GARDNER. This hearing of the Helsinki Commission will come to order. Welcome, and good morning everyone. I'm honored to speak and be here on behalf of Senator Wicker, the Commission's Chairman, and to preside over this morning's hearing.

The Commission is mandated to monitor the compliance of participating states with consensus-based commitments of the OSCE. Today's hearing focuses on the pressing issue of Russian disinformation, and how it undermines the security and human rights of people in the OSCE region.

Disinformation is an essential part of Russia's hybrid warfare against the United States and the liberal world order. As one of our distinguished panel witnesses today wrote in her recent article, "The Russian security state defines America as the primary adversary. The Russians know they cannot compete head to head with us economically, militarily, technologically, so they create new battlefields. They are not aiming to become stronger than us, but to weaken us until we are equivalent."

(1)

Through its active-measures campaign that includes aggressive interference in Western elections, Russia aims to sow fear, discord, and paralysis that undermines democratic institutions and weakens critical Western alliances such as NATO and the EU.

Russia's ultimate goal is to replace the Western-led world order of laws and institutions with an authoritarian-led order that recognizes only masters and vassals. Our feeble response to Russian aggression in Ukraine and their interference in our elections has emboldened the Kremlin to think that such a new world order is not only possible, but imminent.

We must not let Russian activities go with impunity. We must identify and combat them utilizing every tool at our disposal.

I am proud that my home state of Colorado is home to Fort Carson and the 10th Special Forces Group, an elite unit that has been at the tip of the spear in identifying and combating some of these malign Russian activities in the European frontline states. I thank them for their important work and for keeping our nation safe.

To help us lead our discussion today, I am pleased to introduce three distinguished witnesses.

Mr. John F. Lansing is the chief executive officer and the director of the Broadcasting Board of Governors. He joined the BBG as CEO—that's a lot of acronyms—and director in September 2015. Previously, he was the president of Scripps Network, where he is credited with guiding the company to becoming a leading developer of unique content across various media platforms.

Ms. Melissa Hooper is the current director of Human Rights and Civil Society Programs at Human Rights First. Ms. Hooper's research focuses on Russia's foreign policy strategies of spreading Russian influence and undermining democratic institutions in Eastern Europe, and how these strategies intersect with existing autocratic trends.

Ms. Molly McKew is an expert on information warfare and Russian disinformation policies. She currently heads an independent consulting firm, Fianna Strategies, advising governments and political parties on foreign policy and strategic communication. She also has extensive regional experience advising both Georgian and Moldovan governments. She also writes extensively on issues pertaining to Russian information warfare.

We'll begin with Mr. Lansing, who will offer his testimony and inform us what the BBG is doing to counter Russian disinformation in the OSCE region. We'll then move on to Ms. McKew's testimony, where she will discuss information warfare and Russia's activities in this space. And finally, Ms. Hooper will present her analysis of Russian disinformation's influence over the German elections and its potential influence over future elections in Europe.

So thank you very much for your testimony today. I look forward to hearing your discussion as we strive to better understand these serious threats.

Before we begin, though, I will now turn to my colleagues on the Commission—Senator Cardin, Congressman Smith—for their comments.

HON. BENJAMIN CARDIN, RANKING MEMBER, COMMISSION ON SECURITY AND COOPERATION IN EUROPE

Mr. CARDIN. Well, Chairman Gardner, first of all, it's a pleasure to have you here. I miss Senator Wicker, so I——[laughter]

Mr. GARDNER. I'll do my best with Mississippi accents. [Laughter.]

Mr. CARDIN. Senator Wicker is just a great leader on the Helsinki Commission.

But it's great to be here with Senator Gardner. You should all know that I serve with Senator Gardner on the Senate Foreign Relations Committee, and he is a passionate leader on so many issues on the Senate Foreign Relations Committee. So his help here on the Helsinki Commission today is very much appreciated. So thank you for chairing today's hearing.

It's good to be here with Congressman Smith. Congressman Smith is not only the longest-serving member of the Helsinki Commission, but he has been a champion of the Helsinki Commission for longer than I've been in Congress, and I've been in Congress a long time. [Laughter.] So, Chairman Smith, it's good to be here with you.

And today you truly have a distinguished panel of witnesses. We have three witnesses who are truly expert on the subject that we are dealing with today, and that is what Russia's misinformation campaign is all about, the risk factors to the United States and to our values and to our partners, and what we can do to counter that.

I've repeatedly stated that Russia is violating each and every principle of the Helsinki Final Act's guiding principles. Central to Russia's strategy to undermine democratic institutions is a long-running effort to now sow instability through disinformation campaigns. So I hope that we can truly try to understand a little bit more about what they're doing, what Russia's all about, and the impact it has on the United States and our allies, and what we can do with the participating states of the OSCE in order to try to counter these activities.

In a world of rapid technological and social change and upheaval, Russia has not merely grasped the basic applications of the new technology, it has exploited it, and used this openness of our democratic institutions to work against us. I must tell you, we have to admire how Russia has understood the means of communications today, and how they understand our democratic institutions, and how they've used our democratic institutions to advance their own agenda.

We have seen the impact of this disinformation at home and abroad. Russia's disinformation has spread throughout Ukraine, and especially impacted the Ukrainian state's response during the invasion of Crimea and the war in Donbas. We've also seen now the impact of Russia's disinformation in the United States itself. Russia's Facebook users created thousands of fake accounts and flooded the internet with propaganda and lies during the 2016 election period.

This week, as the OSCE convenes Europe's largest annual human rights meeting in Warsaw, Poland, a longtime participant and leading voice in monitoring hate crimes, xenophobia and extreme violence in Russia is under threat. The SOVA Center is now being investigated as "undesirable." This is a painful reminder that Russia's foreign agent law, used to target human rights groups and civil societies in general, is one of Moscow's most insidious global exports.

Russia's disinformation strategy is well funded and it is sophisticated. As we need to be doing a better job in response, the State Department's Global Engagement Center has been tasked in statute with assuming a larger part of this responsibility.

I'm glad to see that the State Department has released resources to the Global Engagement Center. This is something that we had pushed very hard. I want to acknowledge Senator Corker and Senator Graham's efforts in helping us on the Senate side in getting that done. We now need to deal with rigorous oversight of this effort.

The recent Russia sanction bill which was signed into law on August the 2nd included funding authorization to bolster the resiliency of democratic institutions across Europe. I was proud of the role that our committee played with getting that done. It now is important for us to see that it's implemented and oversighted properly.

I must note that this is the Helsinki Commission's third hearing on Russia this year. The Commission has investigated the extensive human rights abuses in Russia and the growing military threat that the Russian state poses.

The scourge of disinformation is a serious and ongoing challenge Russia poses against the global community in spite of its international treaties and commitments. This hearing is extremely important, and I look forward to hearing from our witnesses.

Mr. GARDNER. Thank you, Senator Cardin.

Congressman Smith.

HON. CHRISTOPHER H. SMITH, CO-CHAIRMAN, COMMISSION ON SECURITY AND COOPERATION IN EUROPE

Mr. SMITH. Thank you very much, Chairman Gardner, and thank you for your leadership. And it's just great to see you.

And Ben Cardin and I, we do go back a whole lot of years working on the Helsinki Commission, particularly working against the nefarious Russian enterprises—not just the KGB, but others who have perpetrated horrific human rights abuses over the many years. And so it's great to be with Ben. And I thank him for those sanctions. He and the chairman of the Foreign Relations Committee crafted a very important piece of legislation, which is now law. So thank you, Ben.

The most alarming thing about the Russian media's promotion of untruths and fake news is the extent to which it is coordinated by the Russian Government and put in the service of a doctrine of war, the so-called Gerasimov Doctrine of hybrid war.

Fake news is far from unknown within our society. We deal with it through freedom of speech, which allows it to be disproven, as well as through laws against libel and incitement. Yet, the case is totally different when a foreign government coordinates the production of fake news campaigns as part of a hybrid war against us and our allies.

I'd like to hear from our witnesses today how they think our government can work with our allies to respond to the threat of Russian disinformation and the threat that it poses against Ukraine, Lithuania, Latvia, Estonia, and Georgia in particular. These are countries where disinformation is most fully part and put in service of this hybrid war. How are we responding and how should we respond? And I'm sure we'll get some very good answers from our distinguished panel.

Most importantly, if Russian disinformation is hybrid war against these frontline allies, is our military and the NATO alliance making counter-disinformation part of a hybrid defense against this hybrid war? Over the years—and I mention this because I've done so with Ben on many occasions—we've traveled to Russia many times, including during some of the worst years of the Soviet times. In 1982, my first trip as a congressman was to meet with Jewish refuseniks for a full 10 days in Moscow and in Leningrad. I went back a few years later, then went back again and actually visited Perm Camp 35, where Sharansky and so many other dissidents were held—he [Sharansky] had just left, but others were still there.

We videotaped more than two dozen political prisoners. I'll never forget one of those prisoners said, "Tell Scowcroft I'm here!" He was fingered by Aldrich Ames, and was there and probably would have been killed, and an exchange got him out. But many others were there, and they told their stories. It was the beginning of glasnost and perestroika at the time. But that was still under Soviet times.

Now, I say that because in 2013 I sought to go to Russia after the adoptions were shut down pursuant to a retaliation for the Magnitsky Act, which was absolutely well written and has been put into place. And under Putin, many of us have been not allowed even to travel to Moscow, and I have not been able to get a visa ever since. We could get there during the Soviet times, can't get there now. What does that tell you about the state of Putin's Russia?

And, of course, to punish children, many of whom were already in the pipeline to find homes here in the United States, who would have been well loved, and out of an orphanage in many cases, and well taken care of, and yet that was a shutdown on the part of the Russian Government in retaliation against the Magnitsky Act.

So we really are in a really bad situation with Russia. And I think a hearing like this helps to bring additional light and scrutiny, and most importantly from our witnesses some recommendations on what we could do and do better to combat Putin's aggression.

Thank you.

Mr. GARDNER. Thank you, Congressman Smith.

We've been joined by Senator Shaheen and Congresswoman Moore. Thank you very much for being here today. And if you would like to make additional statements now, please feel free to do so. Otherwise, we'll begin with the testimony and reserve time for opening statements during our question period. Thank you very much.

Ms. MOORE. Thank you, but I'll pass.

Mr. GARDNER. Thank you.

Mr. Lansing, if you'd like to begin.

JOHN F. LANSING, CHIEF EXECUTIVE OFFICER AND DIRECTOR, BROADCASTING BOARD OF GOVERNORS (BBG)

Mr. LANSING. Thank you, Chairman Gardner, Co-Chairman Smith, and members of the Commission. Thanks for inviting me to speak today about the Broadcasting Board of Governors' efforts to counter Russian propaganda and disinformation.

I currently serve as the Chief Executive Officer of the BBG, where I oversee all operational aspects of U.S. international media, including five networks. And those networks are the Voice of America; the Office of Cuba Broadcasting, Radio and TV Martis; Radio Free Asia; Radio Free Europe/Radio Liberty; and the Middle East Broadcasting Networks, which include Alhurra TV and Radio Sawa.

The BBG's mission is to inform, engage, and connect people around the world in support of freedom and democracy. We produce news on all media platforms, and our programs reach 278 million people, unduplicated, on a weekly basis in more than 100 countries and in 61 languages. We increased our audience by 52 million from 2015 to 2016. The BBG provides consistently accurate and compelling journalism that reflects the values of our society: freedom, openness, democracy, and hope.

Today we are encountering a global explosion of disinformation, propaganda, and, frankly, lies by multiple authoritarian regimes and non-state actors such as ISIS. House Foreign Affairs Chairman Ed Royce, referring to Russian propaganda specifically, terms it "the weaponization of information," and I believe that captures the severity quite well.

In Russia, the Kremlin propaganda machine is breathing new digital life into a decades-old strategy of disinformation to influence opinions about the United States and its allies. State-sponsored Russian broadcasters such as RT and Sputnik are expanding their global operations. In fact, earlier this year, a bluegrass radio station on 105.5 FM was replaced by Sputnik, right here in Washington, D.C. The Russian strategy seeks to destroy the very idea of an objective, verifiable set of facts.

The BBG is adapting to meet this challenge head on by offering audiences an alternative to Russian disinformation in the form of objective, independent, professional news and information. I'd like to detail some of our key initiatives for you today.

Since 2014, the BBG has added or expanded more than 35 new programs in Russian and other languages in the former Soviet space. The flagship of this effort is *Current Time*, a 24/7 Russian-language digital network that we launched in February of this year. *Current Time* aims to reach Russian speakers in Russia, the Russian periphery, and around the world. For example, in Stockholm or Jerusalem or Istanbul, Russian travelers can now turn on the TV in their hotel room and find *Current Time* as an alternative to RT.

If they did, here's what they might see:

[A video presentation begins.]

NARRATOR. In a complicated world, it can be difficult to tell what's real. But *Current Time* tells it like it is. It's television for

Russian speakers worldwide, delivering news our viewers care about, information that stands up to scrutiny. *Current Time* brings together top journalists from throughout the Russian-speaking world, delivering a fresh alternative to Kremlin-controlled media. With headquarters in Prague and Washington, and more than 100 reporters on the ground in Russia, Ukraine, Central Asia, the Baltics, the United States and Europe, *Current Time* serves as a reality check with no fake news or spin. *Current Time* is on the air 24 hours a day, seven days a week, with news shows for our European and Central Asian audiences; top-of-the-hour headlines; a daily news digest from Washington and New York; a nightly political talk show, "The Timur Olevsky Hour"; weekend wrap-ups from Washington and Prague; and a weekly analysis, "See Both Sides," that helps viewers tell fact from fiction. Available through cable, satellite, IPTV and online streaming, *Current Time* reaches a potential audience of 240 million Russian speakers across the globe.

And *Current Time* isn't just TV. Its digital platforms draw more than 160 million views on social media, with more than a quarter coming from inside Russia itself. *Current Time* is always on the road with shows that bring our viewers new sensations, sights and ideas; rarely seen documentaries; unexplored places; and ordinary people standing up to extraordinary circumstances, risk-takers and entrepreneurs building a future for themselves and their communities.

This is *Current Time*'s mission: real news, "nastoyashchiye novosti"; real people, "nastoyashchiye lyudi"; in real time, "nastoyashchiye vremya." That's *Current Time* Television.

[The video presentation ends.]

Mr. LANSING. *Current Time* is a first-ever, unique partnership led by Radio Free Europe in Prague along with the Voice of America here in Washington. It's distributed in over 23 countries, having just launched in February, on 59 satellite, cable, and digital distribution outfits. The *Current Time* network produces daily news shows on the United States and global events, including within Russia, and features reports on business, entrepreneurship, civil society, culture, and corruption, and is the leading distributor of Russian-language documentaries from independent Russian documentary film producers. In essence, it provides a Russian-language truthful alternative to the Kremlin's disinformation distortions and lies.

Digital statistics indicate that the *Current Time* network is yielding results already. From January to July of this year, *Current Time* short-form Russian-language videos which are seen on social media within Russia and around the Russian periphery were viewed more than 300 million times, nearly three times the number of views during that same period a year ago. And of those 300 million views, half of those are coming from audiences inside Russia.

Russian disinformation campaigns are truly a global effort, and the BBG recognizes this. Our programming in Russia and the Russian periphery is consumed by over 24 million adults on a weekly basis in 20 languages, including, of course, Russian. We have also deployed a new brand called Polygraph, a joint Radio Free Europe and VOA website that is, in essence, a fact-checker to call out

Kremlin distortions and educate global audiences on media literacy and how to spot fake news.

Russia has jumped to criticize these and other BBG efforts. A Russian state news organization charged that these programs are all produced by "Russian people who put the interests of America above the interests of Russia." Our journalists have also come under attack and are under increasing pressure and intimidation in Moscow.

In addition to the nearly half-billion-dollar combined budgets of RT and Sputnik and other Russian international media, the Russian Government also targets Russian speakers around the world with its vast resources of its domestic state-controlled news and entertainment networks. By contrast, the BBG's FY 2017 budget is $786 million, but spread across 61 languages.

Make no mistake, the United States is confronted by information warfare, and I don't use that term lightly. The good work of our journalists around the world is an essential element of the national security toolkit through the export of objective, independent, and professional journalism, and the universal values of free media and free speech.

There's one thing we won't do, and that's propaganda. Our content is protected by a legislative firewall that prevents the U.S. Government interfering in our editorial decision making. Now, that's important to understand.

I'll close with a quote from Edward R. Murrow, who served as the director of U.S. Information Agency from 1961 to 1964, the predecessor of the BBG. He testified before Congress and said: "To be persuasive we must be believable; to be believable we must be credible; and to be credible we must be truthful."

His words ring true today, more than ever.

Thank you.

Mr. GARDNER. Thank you, Mr. Lansing.

Ms. McKew.

MOLLY K. McKEW, CEO, FIANNA STRATEGIES

Ms. McKEW. Good morning. Thank you, Senator Gardner, commissioners. I am grateful to have the opportunity to share some of my experiences countering Russian information warfare in the past decade.

It's been 10 months since we were informed that an information war is being waged against the American people. Our actions say that we're still trying to decide if this is a real threat or not. We must be clear about what these measures aim to achieve.

First, Russian disinformation is a means of warfare. It's the core component of a war being waged by the Russian state against the West, and against the United States in particular. As I outline further in my written testimony, Russian doctrine is quite clear about the importance, primacy, and aims of information warfare. The Kremlin is operationalizing a fundamentally guerilla approach to total warfare in order to achieve strategic political objectives in a kind of global imperialist insurgency. Within this, the smoke and mirrors of information operations are a primary means of power projection.

Second, the main line of effort in this war is conducted in English. We have failed to secure our information space, allowing our self-defined primary adversary to shape and sometimes control it at will.

Third, we have failed to understand the importance the Kremlin ascribes to these efforts and the resources, formal and informal, that it devotes to them. The Kremlin has built sophisticated information architecture inside our information space. It is constantly reinforced and expanded by the creation and dissemination of considerable amounts of content. It increasingly relies on computational propaganda—artificial intelligence, botnets, and other means of automation, as well as data-driven targeting.

We don't compete offensively or defensively in that war. Yet, in many respects, it is the war that matters most. Information tools are the new super weapons, shifting the fundamental balance of power between adversarial forces.

The Kremlin believes that people are the most exploitable weakness in any system. What the Kremlin sees, for example, is that Facebook is a means of collection and a means of operationalizing information operations effectively and inexpensively: a real-life, free-market, big-brother platform for surveillance and computational propaganda available to any power that is willing to pay for it. Russian information operations have come of age with social media.

Information warfare now plays a significant role in shaping the information environment of our elections and other political discourse in Europe and in the United States. I detail some examples of this in my written testimony, including how Russian-backed information operations in Georgia and Moldova have helped to alter the political landscape.

I want to emphasize this is not about information, but about eliciting behavioral change and about action. Disinformation has purpose. "What did it aim to achieve" is often a more important question than if it is true. Russian information operations are used to activate people and groups in different ways when information is applied on prepared networks. They are integrated into the operational footprint of Russia in Europe and beyond, combining intelligence resources with access to technology and information capabilities, operating with few creative limitations and backed by considerable state resources.

There are a few examples of these from recent news. During the 2016 United States elections, Russian Facebook pages were used to organize anti-immigration protests in the United States. In January, a Russian information campaign sparked protests in Germany about the so-called Lisa case, a false story about a young girl brutalized by refugees. In June, Russian hackers planted a false story in Qatar's news agency which spread and contributed to a major diplomatic rift in Gulf Arab nations. And this year, Russian information operations have aimed to inflame a rift between Poland and Ukraine based on historical debates.

These examples show that Russian information operations aim to deepen divides and amplify unrest, to achieve political outcomes, and to identify enemies for us, internal and external. The Kremlin would rather that we fight ourselves and fight each other than be unified against Russian ambitions and against their interference.

These manipulations don't create tendencies or traits in our societies. They elevate, exploit, and distort divides and grievances that already are present, and they amplify fringe views. Russian information operations are a dark mirror of our weaknesses in which no one really wants to see themselves.

Russia likes to position their doctrine as a response to American actions. It's more helpful to understand that the tools they deploy against us they have used against the Russian people first. They forcibly secured their information space before they attacked ours.

We, as Americans, want to believe this warfare doesn't work on us, that oceans are still a barrier to foreign invasion. But we really have no basis in fact for remaining comfortable with that belief. We do need a new kind of star chamber coordinating our best assets— diplomatic, military, intelligence, industry, nongovernmental, and informal—to counter the information war launched by the Kremlin's power vertical.

I highlight additional measures for securing our information space in my written testimony, but I would like to highlight a few in brief.

First, we need a whole-of-government response driven by a unity of mission. Clear leadership amplifies results. If our government is more open about the threat and the results, media and civil society actors, for example, can follow along and take more action.

Second, we also need an integrated whole-of-alliance approach with our NATO and EU allies. Some, especially Estonia and Lithuania and Ukraine, bring critical capabilities, insight and experience that we need.

Third, irregular warfare, including information warfare, will be fought within our borders. This means we need to rethink authorities. Our most experienced assets shouldn't be boxed out of defending the American people. We need sanctioned irregulars to build defensive and retaliatory capacity in information operations, and a good place to start would be a combination of U.S. Special Forces— who are, by mission, trained to fight unconventional wars—with counterintelligence and independent actors. We must also work with our trusted allies on the geographic front lines of NATO using—as you noted, Senator Gardner—the 10th Special Forces Group, our Europe-aligned group, which brings a range of knowledge and experience in countering Russia to the table.

Fourth, Americans need to be armed with defensive tools. One of these is stronger data and privacy protections that will limit the coercive applications of big data.

Fifth, we need to evaluate how to restrict tools of computational propaganda on social media and whether that is something that we can do.

Finally, we must be far more aware of how the export of Russian capital into our system is influencing critical industries, including tech and big data.

We should never emulate the Russian information-control model. Disinformation has purpose, but fighting it must also have purpose. If we aren't clear about what that purpose is, what we are fighting for and what we believe, then we can't win. But this has been an open battlefield for the Kremlin for more than a decade, and it's not a war we can afford to lose.

Thank you.

Mr. GARDNER. Thank you, Ms. McKew.

Ms. Hooper.

MELISSA HOOPER, DIRECTOR OF HUMAN RIGHTS AND CIVIL SOCIETY PROGRAMS, HUMAN RIGHTS FIRST

Ms. HOOPER. Senator Gardner, Co-Chair Smith, members of the Helsinki Commission, I want to thank you and Chairman Wicker for giving me the opportunity to testify regarding the damage caused to democracy and human rights by Russian disinformation efforts in the United States and Europe, and efforts to combat them.

I've submitted a longer statement. I will highlight a few points here.

Since the election, Congress and other policymakers have become increasingly sensitized to the Russian Government's use of various forms of disinformation. However, I should emphasize that the use of disinformation is not the Russian Government's sole strategy. It is part of a coordinated effort to disrupt and attack liberal norms wherever the opportunity arises, using economic influence, electoral disruption, and the weakening of multilateral institutions, among other strategies.

At Human Rights First, we've documented the effectiveness of these threats in Eastern Europe, including how Russia has contributed to significant backsliding on democracy and human rights in Poland and Hungary, each a NATO ally. Importantly, Hungarian and Polish publics largely disagree with anti-EU and anti-democracy messaging. Nearly 80 percent want to stay in the EU and NATO despite propaganda attacking these institutions. Thus, investments in Eastern Europe that shore up democratic institutions are likely to yield positive results.

In addition to media propagation of disinformation, Russia sponsors government-organized NGOs, or GONGOs, across Europe that contribute their own false and misleading analyses and expert statements. Two Berlin-based Russian-funded organizations are Boris Yakunin's Dialogue of Civilizations and the German Center for Eurasian Studies.

Recently, I conducted research into Russia's use of these think tanks, their contributions to disinformation, and possible links to the far right and ultranationalist Alternative for Deutschland and National Democratic Party in the run-up to Germany's election. What I found was that the Russian-funded think tanks and German far-right parties were putting out similar messages on a number of key topics, including the EU, NATO, the United States, Western democracy, and Western media.

In general, these included attacks on multilateral institutions built on liberal democratic values and indictments of these institutions as serving only elites. Specifically, both argue that Western democracy has been degraded by multiculturalism and Western media is untrustworthy, as well as that the EU and the U.S. are not truly free or democratic.

It bears noting that the reach of these campaigns is at present quite small. Germany seems to be prepared to fend off interference around its upcoming election. German leaders have issued public warnings about potential Russian cyberattacks and disinformation and developed working groups and contingency plans. The German public has therefore been sensitized to the possibility of interference. However, about 3 million Russian speakers in Germany continue to be targeted daily with disinformation about refugees, same-sex marriage, terrorism and defense issues.

Germany has also made some missteps in responding to disinformation. The Network Enforcement Act passed in June essentially forces social-media companies to be the arbiters of what constitutes free speech and what violates German law. This is a dangerous, shortsighted approach and will inevitably force these corporations to rely heavily on censorship.

In January, then-Director of National Intelligence James Clapper said that the attacks that occurred around the U.S. election were a "clarion call for action against a threat to the very foundation of our democratic political system." This threat is not confined to the immediate run-up to elections. Challenges to our democracy are occurring right now, and the U.S. has been slow to respond.

So what do we do? First, I agree with Ms. McKew that the U.S. Government needs to unify around the conviction that Russia used disinformation in the United States. By no means is it the only purveyor of false and misleading information, but it remains a leader in pursuing this phenomenon for political ends.

The U.S. Government needs to present a unified front to European allies, partner with them in combating this threat, and also take a leadership role in crafting a thorough and methodological response.

Second, Congress needs to work with other government bodies, tech companies and civil society to gain a more comprehensive understanding of how disinformation works and can be combated to ensure that all bodies are on the same page and there is a comprehensive plan and approach. It shouldn't rely on shortsighted responses similar to the German law.

Third, much of the U.S. Government's focus has been on messaging and public diplomacy, but we also need mid- and long-term strategies to support democratic institutions and values overseas. For example, funding for the Global Engagement Center is important, but its focus on messaging is only one tool. It isn't by itself a comprehensive response. The best advertisement for democracy and human rights is the demonstration of strong, well-functioning democratic institutions. We need to show people, not just tell them.

On the part of Congress, this means adequately funding democracy and governance programming, including in Eastern Europe, a region we formerly thought had graduated from authoritarianism. For example, the European and Eurasian Democracy and Anti-Corruption Initiative, introduced by a bipartisan coalition, including some from this Commission, would commit $157 million for innovative projects to combat Russian disinformation and influence in Europe, like those that we believe are helping Germany fend off interference in its election.

At a time in which democratic values and institutions are being undermined and challenged directly, we need to invest resources in these mainstays of sustainable security and prosperity. Nations are looking to us for guidance in dealing with this new type of threat. We need to step up and lead.

Thank you.

Mr. GARDNER. Thank you, Ms. Hooper.

I thank you all for your testimony. It's intriguing, fascinating and frightening at the same time. There's a saying in politics that politics is the only place where sound travels faster than light. I didn't come up with that. It's actually printed on the wall in one of the restaurants here in town. But I think it has great meaning, because we're dealing with information here that, once out there, can't be pulled back.

And as children we were taught that if you're on the playground and somebody hits you, it's always the one throwing the second punch who gets caught. But in this case, it's the first one that matters and the second one that no one pays any attention to.

So tell me, Ms. Hooper, Mr. Lansing, Ms. McKew: How do we respond to misinformation in a way that is elevated to the level of that first attention grab of the actual disinformation itself?

Ms. HOOPER. I think you pointed out correctly, Senator Gardner, that just correcting facts after the fact, which is important, is not going to have the same punch. It doesn't have the same breadth and reach. We find in studies that often a correction makes the initial statement more viral, because there is some attempt at censorship. So correcting can be sometimes harmful.

I think there are a couple of ways that we can have that kind of impact. One is something called counter speech. At Human Rights First, we have studied narratives about certain communities, like the Lisa case, and narratives about immigrants and refugees. Putting out stories and narratives by these communities, about these communities, is important. Initiating that communication and putting out information that counters the information we think is going to be falsely presented is helpful.

And then I think that what Mr. Lansing has discussed is media literacy, educating people about being critical of information that could be put out. I think the German Government has done a really good job of that around the election, coming together and communicating to their population to be on the lookout for this. That helps a lot.

Mr. GARDNER. Mr. Lansing or Ms. McKew, would you like to add to that?

Mr. LANSING. Senator Gardner, your point is very well taken. And I think, in terms of the BBG's perspective, it's both an offensive and a defensive strategy. We've really taken to the offensive. You saw the example of *Current Time*, of telling stories and showing documentaries that Russian language speakers, within Russia and outside of Russia, just never see, that they're blocked from seeing. So offensively, we're bringing information and content to audiences that, by the very existence of that content, indicate that they're being blocked from other content.

And then, defensively, Radio Free Europe/Radio Liberty has done a fantastic job with investigative reporting. In fact, they had one investigative report earlier this month that definitively proved that there were Russian armor and tanks in eastern Ukraine based on identifying them visually with a camera and then matching them to tanks and armored personnel carriers seen in Red Square during a parade.

So that kind of offensive/defensive, punch/counterpunch helps us gain some advantage so we're not always on a tit-for-tat trying to correct the record.

Ms. McKew. Just very briefly, to add to what was just said, on our side, and again, focusing on English and not on Russian—which I believe is an important but very separate problem—being clear on the threat and the goals and the purpose of what Russia is doing, especially to the United States, but in our information space more broadly, is extremely important.

Based on polling and other surveys, many Americans don't believe it is happening and don't believe it would have any impact on them. The core of this, which is what's so unnerving, especially if you sit with some of the information—warfare experts in countries that pay a lot of attention to this, is that none of this is the "secret sauce" they all want us to believe it is. It's marketing. It's basic human psychology utilized in new technological ways. But it's very effective in the ways it's being applied, because it's encountering open space to move into. There's nothing coming from our side.

Open-source intelligence projects and investigative journalism and exposing disinformation are very important initiatives, but none of them fill the most critical space, which is narrative and which is storytelling; what is the purpose of what we are doing and how we are delivering that to people. That's an open space right now in which there is very little leadership. For me this is the first step in coordinating what our response needs to be in a way that will be noticed by people, because we've been very absent from it in the past decade.

Mr. Gardner. Thank you.

And the Co-Chair of the Commission, Congressman Smith.

Mr. Smith. Thank you, Chairman.

A couple of questions. First, as you know, recently the news broke that the FBI is investigating Sputnik for a possible FARA violation and that the U.S. associate of RT has been ordered to register with DOJ as an agent of a foreign government. I'm wondering if you thought that was a good step. Will it have positive consequences?

Mr. Lansing. Congressman Smith, I'm aware of that information. It's in the press. There are consequences to anything that would look like an attempt by the U.S. Government to limit or block Russian media in the United States. That's not to say it's not a good idea, but I would suggest that there would be consequences.

We currently have a bureau in Moscow with approximately 50 journalists, mostly RFE/RL and some Voice of America and I worry about a reciprocal response. But at the same time, I think it is a complicated problem, because you have the activities of RT and Sputnik that clearly appear to require some investigation.

Mr. Smith. OK.

Ms. McKew. I might just add to that quickly, amplifying a point that Senator Cardin made in his opening remarks about the information warfare tactics that were applied in eastern Ukraine before the invasion—I think something we really need to look at is what are these organizations, because they're not just media. They're not just reporters.

Starting as far back as the Georgian war in 2008, certainly in Ukraine and in Crimea, the first wave of the war was the arrival of Russian journalists and the establishment of communications from those areas, including completely false video, a narrative that was being established to justify the means of invasion.

So I think it's a very complicated area, the free speech, how-do-we-not-become-Russia-while-responding-to-Russia problem. But these are not standard media organizations, and they are worthy of separate consideration from other things, like BBC, NHK, other state media, which are not at all similar to what Russia does with their state media resources.

Mr. SMITH. One of the concerns that I have—Mr. Lansing, you might want to take this—is there a thought of creating a *Current Time* for China? I co-chair the China Commission with Senator Marco Rubio. My committee, the Human Rights Committee of the Foreign Affairs Committee, that and with the China Commission, I've chaired 62 hearings on China and Chinese human rights abuses.

There are threats to human rights all over the world. Russia and China pose among the most egregious threats to human rights and freedom the world has ever known. And taken together—and they do work increasingly together—I think we are in a very precarious time in our history.

My question would be—especially at a time when CCTV is on a tear, just like the Russians are, to propagandize not just Americans but the world, with the narrative about Xi Jinping's benign benevolence and everything else—I watch CCTV just to stay abreast of what they're doing, their hatred towards Japan and the harkening back to the atrocities committed by the Japanese is a regular feature on that television network—and yet we have been cutting Radio Free Asia slots at the precise time when we should be tripling it.

So my question would be, there seems to be a sense in our government and elsewhere that we give China a pass while we focus on Russia. Now, we should enhance our work against Russia. And I think the work that *Current Time* is doing, I think that's a very, very responsible and responsive attempt to really get the truth out.

But, that said, we are diminishing our capacity to get the truth out in China. As a matter of fact, it is demonstrable. I meet with the folks that run the Radio Free Asia efforts, and VOA has got a similar problem, and they are aghast. They're appalled that we are lessening our ability to tell the truth in that dictatorship. And again, they operate unfettered here in the United States through CCTV and other means. They're even buying Hollywood, as we all know, so that there will not be a criticism leveled against the Chinese dictatorship, because if you want to get your movie, if you want to get your screenplay approved, it will be censored.

And we saw that all happen some years ago—and I had the first hearings, and then several more over the years—on global online freedom, or the lack thereof, where Google and others would voluntarily censor, as the price of admission to that market, what happened at Tiananmen Square. And Google, I swore at them, and Yahoo, Microsoft and others, and I was sickened by the complicity of U.S. corporations to kowtow to Beijing. While the economic interests are nowhere near as robust with Moscow as they are with Beijing, we have enabled dictatorship through these actions.

So *Current Time*—is there something similar planned for China? And again, there seems to be a double standard when it comes to China and our lack of robust broadcasting there and right now, as we meet, the downgrading of Radio Free Asia. I'm the one who offered the amendment to make it 24 hours a day when it was a part time because there's much more that we could be doing in that.

And let me just ask one final question. I have many, but time doesn't permit it. How would all of you assess the European governments' efforts to counter Russian disinformation? Are we working as collaboratively as we could? Estonia, as we know, has made a valiant effort to step up a new Russian-language television station, ETV+, to counter Russian propaganda. But one country alone can't do it. What can be done to coordinate those efforts with our European friends and allies?

Mr. LANSING. Congressman Smith, thank you. I agree with everything you said there.

As far as China, we consider China and Southeast Asia and the China periphery to be on a par with Russia as the top two information battlefields that we're dealing with. Thanks to the successful and positive mark we have from the U.S. Senate for FY 2018, I think we'll be able to enhance and not reduce our RFA coverage, as a matter of fact. And, in fact, we had a special appropriation from FY 2017 that allowed us to develop programming with Radio Free Asia and Voice of America for the first time to create television content for North Korea.

I think we'd all agree that the North Korea situation and the connection with China right now is a key foreign-policy issue for the United States, and we're focusing on that right now. And we've already developed some very interesting programming that counters the narrative in North Korea about what it's like for Koreans living in the United States or for those in South Korea as well.

We're investing in China and its periphery. As with Russia, it's difficult to get television into China and parts of Southeast Asia. We just yesterday went through a situation where we were shut down. Radio Free Asia was shut down in Cambodia by President Hun and we're evacuating our people from Cambodia today. So it's a tinderbox of information complexities and we're facing it head on.

Mr. SMITH. I appreciate it.

Just one final thought, if you could answer those other questions as well. Are you thinking of a *Current Time*-type of effort for China? And again, RFA Mandarin Service is facing a 94 percent cut. I'm encouraged that you're happy with the appropriation.

Mr. LANSING. Yes, the mark will allow us not to have to do that.

Mr. SMITH. Great. Completely not to do it?

Mr. LANSING. Yes. Correct.

Mr. SMITH. That's great.

Mr. LANSING. And the *Current Time* approach is, in essence, the approach we've taken in the last two years that I've been in this chair. To take our five networks and use them together for a greater impact. That's what we're doing, for instance, with the North Korea programming. It's the Voice of America and Radio Free Asia working together, one telling America's story through the Korean diaspora and one telling the story of Koreans in South Korea.

So the answer is "yes," philosophically, to the approach of *Current Time*, which is to use multiple networks to have maximum impact and use taxpayer dollars more efficiently by doing it that way.

Mr. SMITH. Thank you.

Coordination?

Ms. McKEW. Just two quick points on that. I think that there's a range of European efforts that are under way—some are in Russian, some are in other languages—focused in these same areas of investigative journalism countering Russian disinformation. But again, English language resources are absent.

The Baltic example that you mentioned is a good one, where, yes, they're doing more Russian-language broadcasting, but English-language news from the Baltics is still very much controlled by Russia. The primary news sources in English are RT and Sputnik coming out of the Baltics. There needs to be more English-language resources that are not driven by Russian content from a variety of regions in the world.

I think the beginning of how we coordinate that response, something we need to look at more closely is using our military-to-military relationships as the core of this effort. Those are really the steel in our alliance, especially in NATO. In times of political shifts in many countries, and other uncertainties, those really anchor the direction of where we're going. There are tremendous capabilities there that I think we—especially sometimes our diplomatic core—tend to sideline and want to keep out of non-conflict areas, but there's tremendous capability there that can be used in fighting these types of hybrid warfare that we need to utilize more efficiently. Also, I think how do we coordinate everything else is, the United States of America as a full unified government needs to make clear that we're in this fight and that we stand with our European allies on countering Russian aggression in the information space and elsewhere. Right now that is not necessarily clear to our allies in Europe.

Mr. GARDNER. Thank you, Congressman. Thanks.

And for those of you who haven't seen it, some of the content that they have directed toward North Korea is very good, and I would encourage you to have a chance to see that because we're starting to do some very unique things, thanks to the bill that both the chambers passed last Congress that authorized significant funding for some of those new programs. That was one of the good things we did in bipartisan fashion here as it relates to North Korea.

Congresswoman Moore.

HON. GWEN MOORE, COMMISSIONER, COMMISSION ON SECURITY AND COOPERATION IN EUROPE

Ms. MOORE. Thank you so much, Mr. Chairman.

And I want to thank this distinguished panel. I do look forward to having the opportunity to really read your written testimony thoroughly and continue to engage with you on these issues.

I'm going to try not to be as long as my good friend Chris Smith in asking this question. I'm going to work on this. I'm going to try hard. [Laughs.] I'll try hard not to make my question as long as yours, but this is a very, very complicated issue.

I once asked James Clapper, the former director of national intelligence, whether or not he thought that some of the stuff, Ms. McKew, that you say is not secret sauce. It's just basic human psychology and knowing how to manipulate people that has shown that it's effective—asking him if he thought that absent proof that there was actual manipulation of votes or voter rolls and so on, whether or not these sort of psychological messages had an impact on voter turnout or voter choices. He said that the intelligence agencies really weren't equipped or they just really didn't or couldn't make that kind of assessment. I found that very distressing. I can't remember whether it was you, Ms. McKew, or Ms. Hooper that made the point that it's not just diplomacy that we've got to do, but we have to build out our technological infrastructure. I do know that, Ms. McKew, you are the one that made the point that until we all get on the same page and admit that the Russians interfered in our election, that we aren't going to be able to move forward.

So here's my question: Like climate change deniers, is there some sort of drop-dead date that we better come up with in terms of getting our act together, getting on the same page with the Europeans, putting the appropriate assets in the State Department to build out infrastructure and capacity before it's going to be too late and they are really going to infiltrate this space and have it become a virus or germ that we won't be able to reverse it?

Ms. MCKEW. Thank you, Congresswoman, for the thoughts and the question.

I think there's never a "too late," but I think we're really late in responding, and I think for a variety of reasons, policy driven and otherwise, we've been late coming to this fight.

And at this point, I think it's hard not to argue that there have been significant shifts. The erosion of belief that institutional democracy can deliver for representative populations, the erosion of belief that institutions matter in many Western societies, certainly the erosion of the belief that this is something other countries want to pursue, are things that have very much developed over the last decade in parallel with Russian disinformation operations. So interpret that how you will, but I think that our voice needs to be in that space in a way that actually celebrates and represents our values in ways that we haven't seemed to be willing to do in quite some time.

I think that if you're looking at the evaluation of proof of manipulation based on information operations, it's very hard to do, as Clapper suggested. But if you look at shifts in opinion during that same period of time—in particular the period between summer 2015, when we know there was an escalation in Russian activity in our information space—and at parallel shifts in opinion on key issues in certain voting populations in the United States—on issues like free trade there were significant shifts in opinion. I think it's hard to say that what they were doing didn't have an impact. And what we have seen them do in other countries, particularly in countries like Georgia and Moldova and in Ukraine, is focus very much on voter suppression or mobilization, on how to get people to vote or not vote based on who they are.

Ms. MOORE. And to that point, I received several robocalls based on these algorithms and, you know, targeting African-American women, and so on, to suppress the vote. I got a call, clearly a Slavic voice—and they knew that I hadn't voted early—saying it's not too late, you haven't voted, but if you vote for Hillary Clinton, she will deliberately start World War III. Now, you know, being sort of a peacenik-type person, I mean, it's easy to determine from my social footprint that I would be vulnerable to such a message.

And in terms of the whole Facebook thing, targeting its users, we are hearing that they targeted Facebook folks, and anybody who talked about mass incarceration or racial injustice, people were targeted for the super predatory message about Hillary Clinton and news of that fashion. And so I am wondering, is there an opportunity for us—since James Clapper says that our intelligence agencies are not doing it—is there some technology that we have to counter these psychological messages? Is there something you can point to that we could do?

Ms. MCKEW. Absolutely. And I think the points you raise are really good ones. And your point about the campaign targeting and messaging targeting is really important to me, because I think people believe these things aren't happening, because we don't see the same information anymore. The stuff that would have been targeting you on Facebook or in person is not the same things that I would have been getting.

And the first time we saw that used in that specific way, it was in the Georgian elections in 2012, where there were these totally separate information universes created on Facebook to mobilize or demobilize parts of the population in very different ways. So I think the solution to that, there is a technological piece of this.

But the problem is, who's motivated to find it? Industry—that being social media companies and data and technology firms—make a lot of money off of this. They are not interested in shutting this down. And the solution, they seem to be suggesting, is the best way to fight automated content online is to create more automated content online so we can get double the advertising revenue—which I don't think is the best solution when we're talking about persuasive views and people's opinions in between.

But there is certainly an industry role to be played in this, an evaluative role, especially from the Congress, to be played in what can be done to limit the ability of social media to use computational propaganda, and for foreign adversaries in particular to use this for these types of information operations and not just advertising, it's not just selling shoes. This is about aggressively changing the views of individuals, and we need to be aware of that.

Ms. MOORE. Thank you so much.

And thank you, Mr. Chair.

Mr. GARDNER. Thank you.

Ms. MOORE. Well, I have to go back to the "House of the People" to vote. [Laughter.]

Mr. GARDNER. Well, several of us are housebroken already! [Laughter.] Ben and I are housebroken. [Laughter.] Thank you, Congresswoman, for being here.

Senator Shaheen.

HON. JEANNE SHAHEEN, COMMISSIONER, COMMISSION ON SECURITY AND COOPERATION IN EUROPE

Mrs. SHAHEEN. There are some of us that think that's the problem with the Senate. [Laughter.]

Let me begin by thanking each of you for being here, for your testimony and for the work that you're doing in this space. I believe that this disinformation is one of the biggest threats that our democracy faces today. And I think that one of the reasons that we have had trouble developing a whole-of-government approach is because the first thing that really got the attention of the American people was the Russian interference in our elections in 2016, and that was viewed through a partisan lens as opposed to being viewed through an understanding that this is a threat to the foundations of American democracy. It has nothing to do with Republicans and Democrats. It's all about how do we undermine democracy in America and in the West. So I especially appreciate what all of you are doing.

I want to go back to the whole-of-government approach, though, because on the one hand, Mr. Lansing, you talked about the importance of keeping all of the work of the BBG separate from government so it's not viewed as propaganda, which I appreciate and I agree that that's important. But it also makes it difficult, then, to develop a whole-of-government approach.

I've had a chance to ask members of the military about whether we should have a unit in our military that deals with disinformation, and they punted to the State Department. Russia, on the other hand, does have that kind of unit in their military. So the question is, how do we develop that whole-of-government approach given the various interests that we have within our government and the partisan challenges that we still face in terms of dealing with this issue?

Mr. LANSING. Senator Shaheen, I'll start and then defer to the other panelists.

I would just say that I appreciate, and the BGG appreciates, your leadership on the issue of disinformation in the Senate and you keeping it highlighted the way you have. As we think about the BBG—and I discussed earlier the firewall that protects the independence, as you said, so that the content is not viewed as propaganda—that doesn't mean that we're not connected to the Federal Government. We're very much connected. In fact, on our board there are nine board members. It's a bipartisan board, but the Secretary of State, or his designee, serves on our board. And we have regular contact with the State Department. So when we make decisions about where we're going to deploy assets around the world, the decisions are made based on the information that we learn and understand through our colleagues at State and sometimes other agencies. So it's no mistake that we're emphasizing

Russia and the Russian periphery, and China and the China periphery, and ISIS in the Middle East as our top three priorities. Because we understand that, because we stay connected with the U.S. Government. So we can still be involved in a whole-of-government solution. We just have a very unique lane that we operate in. Others could do information programming that would not be in our lane. They could do any number of things.

Mrs. SHAHEEN. Ms. McKew.

Ms. McKEW. Thank you, Senator. And I would also thank you for your leadership on the Kaspersky issue, which is something that has driven many of us crazy for a long time. I'm glad to see we're finally moving forward on getting that out of our government infrastructure, and hopefully the rest of the country as well.

It is a complicated issue. However, I think the one thing we can really look at, right now no single part of our government and no single part of our civil society or industry or anything else wants to take leadership on this because there isn't that center to activity. And when it's created and everybody has to be in the room, suddenly, good things happen. I think the one thing from the Russian side we really can seek to emulate is the informality and creativity that comes from throwing various parts of a mechanism into a room together and seeing what comes out the other side, where you have intelligence talking to industry, where you have military talking to diplomacy in a much more integrated way on the threats, how to respond to them, what to do if you're thinking offensively, certainly.

Mrs. SHAHEEN. But let me just interrupt you for a minute.

Ms. McKEW. Yes.

Mrs. SHAHEEN. Because I think you hit on one of the things that's the real challenge, and that is we don't currently have anybody in charge.

Ms. McKEW. Correct.

Mrs. SHAHEEN. So, again, I've asked the State Department about this. They have not moved forward very rapidly with the funding on their Global Engagement Center, and they were not excited about being the point person on this issue. So who should be in charge? Where should the leadership for this reside, and the direction?

Ms. McKEW. I think until it's clear that the White House believes this issue is something we need to address forcefully, that is a very difficult question. But it needs to be something that's assigned to an individual within our government somewhere to lead this effort.

I think you see a lot of things sitting out there waiting to be used. The GEC is a good example, where Congress has been forcefully saying create this, use this, here's some money. Why aren't you doing anything with it? It's still sitting there. In the Pentagon, there's an entire part of the Pentagon that deals with information operations. What are we doing with them right now? The Marine Corps just created a new directorate of information operations. Why aren't they coordinating with the other military branches that work on these things? Again, special forces have great capacity in Military Information Support Operations, and none of these are coordinated. They're all sort of drifting around. And again, none of these things have any mandate to look at what is happening inside the United States, coordinate with counterintelligence.

And there was a really good piece in Politico last week by Asha Rangappa talking about this, that there's no authorities for counterintelligence to look at social media or counter, you know, sort of aggressive, hostile information operations within the American information space. There's just a lot of rethinking that needs to be done in terms of authorities and how we respond. And until there is some sort of coordination body, I just don't know how we get to that answer.

But certainly, the Senate and the Congress can provide leadership on this by sort of forcefully mandating that we move in this direction and that there is somebody within the U.S. Government looking at legal authorities, sort of organizational authorities, structure of political will. And even if everybody doesn't show up, maybe you get enough people in a room to have a critical mass to move forward, or at least to use what is already there that we are currently not coordinating and not utilizing well.

Mrs. SHAHEEN. Thank you. I know I'm out of time, but can I just get Ms. Hooper to respond to this as well?

Ms. HOOPER. Sure, very quickly. I think that we have seen some leadership coming from Congress where the White House and the Secretary of State have left a gap, and I would encourage more of that leadership in this space, in terms of looking at the funding for democracy programming in the State Department. And again, holding hearings and raising this issue repeatedly, I think that's where we are seeing leadership. We're going to need more of that, but it's going to also need to coordinate with technology companies, for example, and also civil society, where there's expertise as well.

Mrs. SHAHEEN. Thank you.

Thank you, Mr. Chairman.

Mr. GARDNER. Thank you.

Senator Cardin.

Mr. CARDIN. I think Senator Shaheen is raising some extremely important points. The Congress has tried to intercede to focus on this issue, to coordinate the activities of various agencies. I must tell you, I've been extremely impressed by the work in our intelligence community in this area. They've been very active, and they have shared that information not just with the Congress but with our friends around the world. So there's been some strong coordination on the intelligence front as to what is happening.

Where we haven't seen the attention is on how you counter it, how you protect and counter. That's where I think we have really not seen the work. I've had some meetings with our colleagues in NATO and the EU to try to energize better cooperation. Congress has authorized funds for international efforts. Those funds were just recently released. There's also—and Senator Gardner and I have talked about it—in our oversight functions there really hasn't been a clear responsibility. The Senate Foreign Relations Committee has, I think, the principal responsibility here. There are other committees involved. But we haven't really focused on that aspect of it. And we're talking about perhaps a way of reorganizing some of the work in our permanent committees to deal with this.

The OSCE is the largest regional organization in the world. It has an overwhelming majority of its members who are of like mind as to what Russia is doing and that it is dangerous to our security, and we need to be better defended and have an offensive way to counter their misinformation. We all understand—well, at least those of us that have been on the Helsinki Commission understand—the bureaucratic challenges of the OSCE, particularly Vienna. But we also know about the hope within the Parliamentary Assembly that we are able to get pretty direct action against perpetrators that are against the principles of the Helsinki Final Act.

So my question is, is there an avenue within the OSCE, within the Helsinki Commission, where we can organize countries of like mind to more effectively deal with the preparation for what Russia is doing, but also how we can have platforms to counter that misinformation. I appreciate, Mr. Lansing, what you're doing, but I would think that it would be more helpful if we also had the input and cooperation of more and more countries that recognize the danger of this disinformation campaign. How could we more effectively utilize the U.S. Helsinki Commission and the OSCE?

Mr. LANSING. We would be very open to working with our friends and allies in this. We do have an organization called the DG7, which brings together the state broadcasters of many of our allies—Japan, Australia, Germany, France, the U.K.—and we meet once annually to compare research and goals and see how we can help one another in various parts of the world. But I think that type of approach is something that we'd be very favorable towards.

Mr. CARDIN. Any other suggestions on how we can get other countries working with us more effectively to recognize the threat—and the intelligence information is there. They know what's going on. But what I have not seen, is a coordinated effort among countries to affirmatively defend ourselves and to counter what Russia is doing.

Ms. MCKEW. I would agree with you on that, and I think that the OSCE can potentially play a role. Sometimes the issue tends to be that the Russians can mess up what is happening within the OSCE, but if there is the ability to build a like-minded group, particularly one that can bring together the people we think of as donors in this space—the U.S., the U.K., Swedes, others who have been forthcoming with resources to fight Russian disinformation in a variety of projects—with the countries that are sort of frontline partners who don't really have the resources to contribute to this fight but they have the expertise and the experience and the manpower and the history to understand what is happening in more clear ways, that could be extremely useful. I think that would be a very useful effort.

Ms. HOOPER. Can I just echo? I know that Dunja Mijatovic, who was the former special representative on freedom of the media in the OSCE, did put out a paper on combatting disinformation and was pulling together groups of journalists, for example, to develop strategies and talk about strategies within the OSCE space, and I think that's pulling on what Ms. McKew noted, that there's a lot of expertise in the OSCE among countries that had been affected by Russian disinformation in various ways that are on the frontlines. But you'll note that, then, Ms. Mijatovic's term was cut short because there were political reasons that the Russian Government was involved in trying to cut short her term. So I think that there is of course that risk, but there is the opportunity as well because there are many like-minded countries within the OSCE.

Mr. CARDIN. Well, a consensus organization is always restricted as to taking formal action, but the OSCE has a long history on freedom of the press and opportunities, and where we can use that in human rights, where we can showcase what's going on as far as misinformation. I would just urge us to use those opportunities.

I mentioned the human rights meeting that takes place annually in Poland. We'll have our winter meetings in Vienna, of the Parliamentary Assembly. Our annual meeting in July is in Berlin. There are opportunities for sidebar meetings. There are opportunities for action. The Parliamentary Assembly works by majority—it's more democratic than how Vienna works—we could get some things and we could put a spotlight on what's going on and we could have a forum to recognize that we must be more effective in sharing strategies to defend against Russian disinformation. I just think there are ways that we can do this, and I think you all can be very helpful to us in putting that together.

Mr. LANSING. Senator Cardin, I think that's a really terrific suggestion. We're actually hosting the DG7 meetings here in Washington in December. That will include the French, the British, the Germans, the Dutch, Japanese, Australian, and we'll put this on the agenda for that meeting.

Mr. GARDNER. Thank you, Senator Cardin.

Senator Whitehouse.

HON. SHELDON WHITEHOUSE, COMMISSIONER, COMMISSION ON SECURITY AND COOPERATION IN EUROPE

Mr. WHITEHOUSE. Thank you, Chairman. And thank you to all the witnesses.

Just to be clear, is everybody in agreement that the Russians interfered in the last election?

Mr. LANSING. Yes.

Mr. WHITEHOUSE. Yes, yes. Three for three. OK. Are all of you familiar with the publication "The Kremlin Playbook," and the publication "The Kremlin's Trojan Horses," by CSIS and the Atlantic Council, respectively? Yes, yes, yes?

Mr. LANSING. I am not.

Mr. WHITEHOUSE. You're not. OK. Are the two of you that are familiar with those two publications, what's your opinion of them? Are they reliable, complete, trustworthy? Do you agree generally with the findings that they made?

Ms. HOOPER. Yes, I think that they lay out a large number of the strategies that we've referenced today that Russia is using throughout Europe, also in the United States.

Mr. WHITEHOUSE. Ms. McKew?

Ms. MCKEW. I would agree with that. I think they do show partial strategies very effectively. I think the Kremlin has a wide range of tools that they use. And I think one of the narratives that we don't pay enough attention to, and in particular in the political parties that the Kremlin is sort of cultivating relationships within

Europe and elsewhere, it's no longer the Marine Le Pen model as much as it is the "soft on Russia" model. And I think we need to be far more aware of this.

You especially see it on social media, the sort of middle rank of sort of Western journalists hanging out in Moscow, and others who propagate this narrative of, OK, Russia is bad, but America is worse, and America should know better, so it is much worse. And anything you do to respond to Putin means you're a Russophobe and it just makes them stronger and proves his point. This is very effective in integrating its way into the American media environment, particularly in graduate students, it turns out, and we just need to be aware of that and be very aware that what they're cultivating now is not pro-Russian views as much as, "don't look over here, don't look at the man behind the curtain."

Mr. WHITEHOUSE. So as we try to prepare ourselves to defend against Russian interference in the 2018 and 2020 elections, I'd like you to comment on two potential vectors for Russian interference. One is the ability of people who seek to influence elections to spend money—indeed, very significant amounts of money—in American elections without attribution, while remaining anonymous. Presumably, we all agree that that's not a good thing in terms of defending against foreign interference in American elections. How serious a vulnerability is it, on a scale of 1 to 10? Let me just go down the row.

Ms. HOOPER. I think that is a serious vulnerability. There might be something that may be more serious, so I'll give myself a little bit of room and say eight or nine.

Mr. WHITEHOUSE. OK. But very serious?

Ms. HOOPER. But yes, quite serious.

Because that is precisely how you see Russian funding going to far-right and far-left disruptive parties throughout Europe. I can speculate to other places, but I know that there is quite a bit of funding in Europe. You have gatherings of disruptive parties going to St. Petersburg to meet. It's Russian money that is making this happen. And so I think that we need to guard against that here.

Mr. WHITEHOUSE. Mr. Lansing, you don't need to give a number. Perhaps that was asking too much. But slightly, very, extremely? How serious is that as a vulnerability?

Mr. LANSING. Having been in the media business for four decades, it's clear that money is what drives results on any platform, so I'd say extremely.

Mr. WHITEHOUSE. Ms. McKew?

Ms. McKEW. And I would agree with that. Just briefly, the new ideology of export from the Kremlin is kleptocracy, and money is the means of recruitment. It is the means of influence and infiltration. We're not paying enough attention to that. I'm pretty hardline about this, but there is very little money coming from Russia that is clean or not connected to Kremlin interests and motivations, and we need to be far more aware of how that works in our societies.

Mr. WHITEHOUSE. One of the things that is happening around the world—and this will be the second part of my question—is that companies are cleaning up the corporate transparency problem. Unfortunately, that leaves the United States of America in very bad company of misbehaving countries who have not cleaned up corporate transparency.

And in that light, could you comment on the nature of shell corporations that you can't see who is truly behind as a danger or a vulnerability in our elections to Russian influence? Same question as the last one, but instead of unattributed money this is corporations who you don't know who is behind the shell.

Ms. HOOPER. I am grateful that you mentioned that because I think that is an area where the U.S. has allowed Russian money, allowed other types of corrupt kleptocratic funds to come into the U.S. And this not only harms our own system, it harms our reputation as we try to portray our values as democratic values overseas. I think that that is precisely where the U.S. needs to be putting attention when it is thinking about things like Russian disinformation and Russian influence.

How are our laws allowing this to happen? Shell corporations is definitely one area where I think that there's a great vulnerability.

Mr. WHITEHOUSE. Mr. Lansing, agree or disagree?

Mr. LANSING. I agree with Ms. Hooper and have nothing to add.

Mr. WHITEHOUSE. Ms. McKew?

Ms. MCKEW. The anonymous movement of money through various financial systems is an extreme challenge to us. And I think in particular looking at the United States, the movement of Russian money into our system is not about buying real estate and yachts. It's about buying us. And we need to be very clear about that.

Mr. WHITEHOUSE. Final question—and this takes, Ms. Hooper, your point. Let me posit a hypothesis—and it's obviously going to be not accurate specifically—but posit that there is a corrupt world in which Russia is a very prominent player, basically a criminal enterprise that happens to also enjoy nativist sentiment and nuclear weapons, and has occupied a country, and on the other side, "rule-of-law land." So if you generally were to divide the world between "corrupt land" and "rule-of-law land," what are the ways in which "rule-of-law land" is actually facilitating corruption and kleptocracy in "corrupt land?" And how important is it for us to try to clean that up? And is that a sensible way to be thinking about this international rivalry, or contest?

Ms. Hooper, you first.

Ms. HOOPER. Yes, it is a sensible way. As was mentioned earlier, I think corruption and the flow of Russian corrupt money is the main way that Russian influence leaks into other countries, and that is through buying individuals, buying corporations, buying property. Here, it's also through sending children to universities, or allowing corrupt officials to vacation in the United States, sometimes. There are so many ways that we see corrupt money flowing freely.

Mr. WHITEHOUSE. Is there an incentive for people who've stolen a lot of money in "corrupt land" to move their money into "rule-of-law land" so that they're not in turn robbed by the next bigger thief?

Ms. HOOPER. Yes, of course, because there are rules to protect it.

Mr. WHITEHOUSE. That's how they protect themselves from being robbed by the next bigger thief in "corrupt land," correct?

Ms. HOOPER. Yes, that's right. And I believe that a recent statistic said that more than half of Russian corrupt money is not in Russia.

Mr. WHITEHOUSE. And what role do American law firms, accounting firms, advisers, and other entities play in facilitating that?

Ms. HOOPER. Law firms, accounting firms, lobbying firms are all advising kleptocrats on how best to take advantage of the rule-of-law system we have here.

Mr. WHITEHOUSE. OK. I think my time is probably expired, but I appreciate the witnesses being here and I appreciate the theme of this hearing. Very well done.

Thank you.

Mr. GARDNER. Thanks, Senator Whitehouse.

Ms. McKew, you had experience with people who witnessed this firsthand. It was about them. They went through it. Could you talk about some of the effects it had on the thought process of individuals that said this misinformation was aimed at in Georgia and other places that you've had experience in—what it was like to go through that, the pressures it created, how they dealt with it, and the experiences that you glean from that that we should learn from?

Ms. McKEW. It's a really interesting question, and I think it gets back to this point that it's very difficult for disinformation, but in particular Russian operations, to create new divides or a new part of the landscape, but it's very easy for them to exacerbate and exploit what's already there. And in Georgia in 2012, that space was very much the halted reforms in the justice sector, the concerns about what was happening in the expansion of rule of law in the country, and that was the sort of wiggle room to get into in terms of creating this black PR narrative of the "bloody nine years of the rule of Saakashvili," which I think most people would disagree is truth. Certainly, there were issues with the Saakashvili government, but "bloody nine years" is not a valid representation of what happened during that time when significant things transformed toward democracy in the country.

But it was this targeting. The government didn't know any of this was happening. Anybody who on Facebook or other social media had sort of liked anything from that side would be excluded from the operations that were going on. So there was this very divided view of the country that evolved over the year when these operations were applied. Toward the end, when you had not just a narrative of what way do we want the country to go, what didn't you like, are you disadvantaged compared to others, but the things right before the election, the supposed prison rape tapes that were put out, and the night of the election when there was this fake story, which was much later debunked, about this dead baby that had been found in a well that they claimed the government or the ruling party had killed—but all of this was playing out in real time across the information network that had been built by Bidzina Ivanishvili, whose money is Russian, and very much backed by Russian information enterprises.

And I think that the effect this had on people—on Georgians in particular, who after the war in 2008, there was this sense of the existential threat in the country. And it's exhausting. It's exhausting for any country to have to think all the time about invasion, turmoil, takeover. And all of this sort of exploited that sense of, "wouldn't it be great if things could just be normal again," but it created this environment of fear and the potential for violence that really suppressed part of the vote, and elevated another part of the vote in ways that I think really shifted the outcome of what that election was. And I think that's fairly easy to pull out.

In Moldova, it's a little bit different. It's a very divided country, the Russian-speaking part versus the Romanian-speaking part. But it is such a terrible information environment, where four or five national channels are controlled by the oligarch who controls the country, who is nominally pro-European, but his channels are the ones that promote all the pro-Russian propaganda in the country. The courts that he controls are the ones that have laundered the $40 billion of Russian money through Moldova into the EU. Within that environment, the way that they control the country is through division, through saying you have no choice but maintaining these divisions, or the Russian-speaking population would be disadvantaged anywhere else, the Romanian-speaking population would be disadvantaged with any other thing going on. And it's this constant churn that is used to control what people think their options are, and that's why everybody's leaving the country. But that constant maintenance of these narratives is very difficult, it's all about information, and it's information used to mobilize people in specific ways.

Mr. GARDNER. But when you look around the globe and you look at Europe, you look at Germany, look at France, the United States, our efforts, is somebody doing this better than we are? Is somebody getting it right? Is there more policy in place somewhere that's having a better effect than we are? France, during their election, was able to fight back a little bit. Can you explain how—and let me hear from all three of you.

Ms. MCKEW. I think that there are countries that watch and assess this problem better than we do. But in terms of response, I'm not sure that anybody really has anything yet, other than happenstance. I think part of what happened in the French election, there's sort of a cultural resilience to slander and scandal that we don't have as Americans.

There's a big language issue. The way the Russians talk about this constantly is the "linguistic hegemony of English," which is the thing they're trying to break with RT and Sputnik. But they're not wrong about that, which is English is the language of the internet. So when they do these operations, in terms of the information space, in English, we are the echo chamber they're pointing at, and everything just kind of bounces around. They don't do that much in French. There's not as much effort applied. Same in German, although mostly what their avenue of disruption is right now is they're targeting the Russian population, the Russian-descended population within Germany, and then other things. But it works better in English, and that is why I think you've seen the results that are Russian connected on Brexit, on the American election, where there just feels like there's more going on that we haven't seen.

Ms. HOOPER. I wanted to add a quick point. I think that both France and Germany have done better in one respect: French media was able to agree that they would not cover the hacked information that was released. And so the media there agreed not to do that, and I think that that was a significant step there. In Germany, you have Angela Merkel meeting with experts on disinformation right after the U.S. election, saying what is this, what do we do with it, and then there's a coordinated government-wide task force that has developed contingency plans around this election. If there's a drop of disinformation on a campaign that occurs, what do we do, how are we going to respond? They all know. And there's even a secondary voting computerized system that's been set up in case their primary computerized system is attacked. There are contingency plans. In addition to informing the public this might happen, they're specifically informing themselves and taking action.

Mr. GARDNER. And I thank you for that.

Senator Shaheen.

Mrs. SHAHEEN. Yes, I'll do a third round with you.

Mr. GARDNER. Thank you. [Laughter.]

Mrs. SHAHEEN. Lest someone think that Americans are immune to this kind of disinformation, I can tell you that in the public forums that I have done in New Hampshire, I have had in each one someone speak up with the exact Russian narrative on the issue that's being raised, whether it's Syria, whether it's the elections, whatever it is. And most of the people who have done that have been people who have been educated. They have been people who you think, gee, they ought to be able to recognize the difference. So the question of media literacy is the one that I really wanted to get at. What responsibility does the media here have to point out, as opposed to just repeating some of these narratives, and what more can we do to address that issue so that there's—among responsible media in the country, an effort to really take a look at this?

That's you, Ms. Hooper.

Ms. HOOPER. I don't want to say that the media is the problem, because I believe that media in the U.S. is really a symbol of who we are and what we are, and the fact that——

Mrs. SHAHEEN. I agree, and I'm not suggesting that the media's the problem.

Ms. HOOPER. I understand. But I agree with you that there seems to be a tendency in the U.S. for us to go to the shiny object, and that includes with our media. And sometimes the shiny object is something that has nothing to do with substance or with facts. I do feel like media has a responsibility, and a raising of that issue and a highlighting of the ethics responsibility of journalists and of media, I think, would be helpful and important for us now.

Mrs. SHAHEEN. Mr. Lansing, as someone who's come out of that world?

Mr. LANSING. Yes, not speaking as the BBG CEO but just in my experience having been a journalist myself and a news director, I thought it—first of all, I take your point very much, and I thought it was interesting to watch the evolution of the coverage last year. When you'd be watching one of the cable television networks and you'd hear something said that was empirically untrue, and the

moderator would just let it go right by. And then after a while—
and I think CNN was a leader in this, and the others came along—
you saw them becoming a little more aggressive to call something
out as being untrue, or even to say that's empirically false. So I
think it took the media a little bit of time to catch up with what
was a blast of disinformation that seemed to come out of nowhere.

And to your point, I think the media has a responsibility in the
best tradition of media to offer perspective and context. And part
of perspective and context is helping an audience understand, or a
media consumer understand, how to be a smart consumer of media.
And I think more could be done to do that.

Mrs. SHAHEEN. So how do we encourage that among the media?
One of the examples that I use that I'm sure you all heard was the
story on social media that got picked up by Fox News and repeated
and then got repeated by the President, and then finally they had
to debunk it and say, oh, no, that was a Russian-planted story. But
how do we get the media to police itself on these issues?

Ms. McKew?

Ms. MCKEW. It's an interesting question, and I think part of this
gets back to the post-2016 election in particular. Now everyone is
a Russia expert. And people commenting on Russia and the purpose of Russian information operations on the news are often the
person who just commented on whether or not the next Supreme
Court justice is going to be good for the country. And I have no
commentary on the next Supreme Court justice, but I do think that
we need to be careful about how we are applying expertise in
media, absolutely.

But part of it is raising awareness of this narrative issue. What
is the Russian narrative here trying to achieve? How does it do
that? How does it work? And part of it is building awareness in the
commentariat but also in journalists about those things. I have had
more than one argument in the past two years with good friends
of mine who are good, extremely good aggressive credible journalists who have written a story that is clearly Russian
disinformation. And if you poke at them and say, what is this story
that is demonizing Ukraine, amplifying some bit of Russian narrative from the Middle East, whatever it is, and you can finally get
back to whatever the source was, it's just, "it seemed like a good
story, so we're going to write it."

But the Russians are very sophisticated about how they get information in front of us. They use proxies, they use secondhand
people, they use pass throughs, they use people who've been in the
United States for a long time. The outreach to journalists and to
others, to think tank experts, to academics in particular is a long-
term effort. They're very good at introducing information into our
systems, in journalism, in intelligence in other countries, and we
need to be more aware of how that information moves and what
it aims to achieve.

I think there's also another piece of this in the media space, particularly on social media which is sort of algorithm based, and the
financial models of these companies is, on basically creating an in-
finite confirmation bias system. I had this amazing conversation
with a Facebook guy a couple years ago when he was lamenting
that he doesn't understand Washington or how divided our infor-

mation spaces have become. Why do we think this is so bad? And I looked at him and said, maybe because everybody's reality is curated for them on Facebook. And it had never occurred to him that this was a problem at all. The model where social media decides you want to see this, so we're going to show it to you—if you and I searched something on Google right now too, we would get totally different results sitting 10 feet apart in the same room. This needs to be something we're looking at, because it's giving us inaccurate views of the world as a means of selling things sometimes, but it's not helping us in terms of building sort of cognitive resistance against disinformation.

Mrs. SHAHEEN. Thank you.

Thank you, Mr. Chairman.

Mr. GARDNER. Senator Whitehouse, if you care.

Mr. WHITEHOUSE. Thank you, Chairman.

Ms. McKew, I left off with a question to Ms. Hooper about the role of U.S. lawyers and accountants and lobbyists and advisers and banks in facilitating the protection of resources stolen in "corrupt land" so that they can find sanctuary in the safety of "rule-of-law land." And I'd like to have you comment on the same question, if you recall that.

Ms. McKEW. Yes, absolutely. I think the point you hit on is the right one, which is it's the exploitation of our system that is the thing the Russians are really great at in many regards, particularly in finance. I think the initial way—the first round of accountants and others who became engaged in this are the same guys who are laundering money for people getting divorced and, you know, it's the normal movement of—or hiding of—corporate assets, hiding of personal assets that regular non-kleptocratic individuals and companies engage in. That is the infrastructure into which kleptocratic money is moving in Russia and other places.

Mr. WHITEHOUSE. And that's in part because if you leave the money in "corrupt land," the next bigger thief can steal it.

Ms. McKEW. It's totally vulnerable, absolutely. And you can't use it.

Mr. WHITEHOUSE. And you can't use it.

Ms. McKEW. It's not good for anything. You have to get into legitimate banking systems, yes.

Mr. WHITEHOUSE. So you've got to move it over.

Ms. McKEW. Yes.

Mr. WHITEHOUSE. And in that sense, how important is that network of "rule-of-law land" support entities—the lawyers, the bankers, the accountants—in actually making the corruption in "corrupt land" pay off for the people who engage in it?

Ms. McKEW. They are allowing corruption to be profitable and allowing it to bleed into our systems in ways that we are not aware of.

Mr. WHITEHOUSE. And the final question on this takes us back to a point that presidents have made about our country, that we are a little bit different than other countries. We are an exemplary nation that, as one said, the power of our example has always mattered more than any example of our power. And from Jonathan Winthrop to Ronald Reagan, we have talked about the United States of America as being a city on a hill. And in our national hymn we talk about that alabaster city is supposed to gleam. So what are the costs? A, do we get value in this world, in your view, out of being that exemplary nation? And, B, what is the effect on that value of allowing ourselves to become the functionaries of kleptocrats in "corrupt land?"

Ms. Hooper?

Ms. HOOPER. Yes, there is value. I can tell you, having worked for years overseas, in Russia, in Central Asia, in the Caucasus, everywhere I work, even when I express concern about our criminal justice system or something that's happening in the United States, my colleagues would tell me no, your system works, but, no, we are looking to your system. This is what I've heard everywhere. So, yes, there is of course value in this.

Mr. WHITEHOUSE. Ms. McKew.

Ms. McKEW. Of course I would agree that there is tremendous benefit to the "city on the hill" remaining the city on the hill. I think that the construction of the post-World War II architecture, in terms of security and economic integration with Europe, the transatlantic alliance is what has made us an enormously prosperous, secure and influential nation in the world. So the idea that this is not something we benefit from is——

Mr. WHITEHOUSE. It's not just that we have more rockets and missiles than other people. The power of our example matters.

Ms. McKEW. The power of our example is enormously important. And if you ask any of our allies, especially the newly freed states from the post-Soviet space, they still don't get why we don't understand this and why we're not fighting for it in the way that they did and that they have.

Mr. WHITEHOUSE. In the battle of ideas and ideologies that make up our world, how does that power of our example fare when we are engaged in systematic support for the kleptocrats of corrupt land?

Ms. McKEW. I think one of the arguments I've tried to make the most in the past year in particular, but also before, is the ways in which Russian money influences us. I'm sure other countries have the same issues. But it's not always——

Mr. WHITEHOUSE. I mean, my question is in terms of reputation.

Ms. McKEW. Yes, absolutely. But it's not always—it's the way in which we silence ourselves to keep the flow of money open. At a conference in Tallinn earlier this year, there was a great panel of European bureaucrats talking about the problems of Russian blah blah and I asked them: if we know this is what the money is achieving in our systems, in our politics, in our media, et cetera, why don't we do anything about it? And the answer was, "We're all making too much money and nobody's going to take the hit."

We see the impact that this has had in the U.K. in particular. In London, there's a huge bastion of keeping illicit Russian funds in place, and in other places as well. You see in Europe the ease with which politicians move straight from politics into Russian business. We should not believe that there is any less influence with Russian money in Washington. The number of advisers around political campaigns, around political parties in general who are taking Russian money, representing Russian interests—and even if they're not advocating for Putin, they're not going to say anything critical because they want to keep getting that check—is an enormous problem, and one I find very disheartening. There is a lot of Russian money, and the way that it works here and influences Washington in particular is something we don't pay attention to very much.

Mr. WHITEHOUSE. Thank you, Chairman.

Mr. GARDNER. Thank you, Senator Whitehouse.

The Zapad exercises are starting in Belarus today. A hundred thousand Russian troops, it's estimated, will be in Belarus as a part of this exercise. Are you seeing anything, hearing anything in regards to disinformation surrounding this, and what have you seen, and how is it being countered?

Ms. MCKEW. I think, from the Russian side, they're doing their usual "it shows our tremendous military might, and yet it's a nothing-burger, don't pay any attention to what's going on over here" routine. They claim it's far smaller, 13,000 troops.

Mr. GARDNER. And it is a hundred thousand or—yeah, right.

Ms. MCKEW. For our Baltic allies, it's an enormous mobilization with a tremendous amount of forward-deployed equipment moving into Belarus in advance of the exercises, all of which was documented by rail schedules. In particular, there's a lot of anxiety about what this means. In the U.S. operational mindset, we have this challenge of divided geographic commands. If you're sitting in Moscow and looking out, the Baltics, Ukraine, the Middle East, and North Korea are kind of all in the same ring of operation. There's a lot of anxiety that as tensions in North Korea escalate, that creates more opportunity for Russia to move in the West if they decide to try to test NATO or challenge other security infrastructure. This year feels different. There's real anxiety about what's happening in terms of whether this just means that Russian equipment is never moving back out of Belarus, like maybe the men leave but the stuff stays.

Maybe they move some of it to Kaliningrad. Nobody's really sure. But it definitely has more of that pre-2008, pre-2013 sentiment than not, I would say.

Mr. GARDNER. One of you talked a little bit about education and being taught what to look out for. Journalism school, reporters, you're looking at this kind of a campaign out of Russia. Is this taught in class? Is this something that you can teach? How do we provide this education? Is this something that needs to happen as part of professional development going forward? How does this work?

Mr. LANSING. I'm privileged to be on the National Advisory Board for The George Washington University School of Media and Public Affairs, and their leader, Frank Sesno, immediately, within a week after the election last year, started conducting forums that brought all the students together with people like Sean Spicer and others that were heavily involved, and there were really rich and deep conversations going on at the GW campus about what happened and how to think about journalism after the 2016 election. So I'm seeing, at least at GW—and I'm sure they're not alone—a push in academia, in terms of journalism schools, to make sure there are lessons learned, particularly just going back to the point of the context that's missing, to Senator Shaheen's point, about understanding how to be a better consumer of news, and also how to be a better journalist to help people be a better consumer of news.

Mr. GARDNER. Yes, and by then, though, the vast number of consumers of that information are going through college and they're not receiving that in class. So they've gone through high school, how do we make sure that we have critical reading, critical thinking skills that are appropriate in this new world of 24-hour/7-day-a-week access to information, so that we are making sure that people need to question what they read, and make sure they know where the information is coming from and make their opinions on their own and have not somebody else's being fed to them?

Mr. LANSING. Completely agree that it would need to expand beyond just the journalism schools and really just anyone who's going to be a consumer of media needs to have a more astute method for understanding what they're hearing or seeing or reading, and where it's coming from.

Mr. GARDNER. Senator Shaheen.

Mrs. SHAHEEN. Thank you.

Well, I would argue that media should include social media as well.

Mr. LANSING. I agree.

Mrs. SHAHEEN. Because one of the reasons that we're in this place is because we have this whole new technology that's social media.

Mr. LANSING. Yes.

Mrs. SHAHEEN. I want to go back—Ms. Hooper, you talked about Russian support for right-wing organizations in Germany, and you all referenced their support for parties, different political parties, right-wing. Do we have any evidence that Russia has supported right-wing groups in the United States, and white supremacist groups, neo-Nazi groups here?

Ms. HOOPER. I don't have any evidence. There is a researcher, Casey Michel, who focuses primarily on this issue. Russia has gathered separatist groups—for example, California separatists, Texas separatists—and there is evidence that the websites of California separatists and Texas separatists are supported by Russian institutions. But for general political parties, I can't say that I have evidence. You have a lot of similar argumentation, but, again, I want to make evidence-based arguments, and I don't have evidence for that.

Mrs. SHAHEEN. Sure, yeah—no, that's what I'm asking.

Ms. McKew, have you seen anything?

Ms. McKEW. Yes, is the answer. And, you know, it's not that anybody can prove financial connections or anything else, but in terms of rhetoric and overlap of operations, there's a lot of integration between the Russian information architecture in some of these actors who have been represented on Russian state media.

Russia hosts a lot of conferences. Some are these separatist groups in which the Texas, Alaska and California separatist movements have attended in the past, in Crimea and other exciting places. But on the idea of the white supremacist groups, ultranationalist groups, the traditional values groups, Russia's been very aggressive in cultivating relationships with these groups—sometimes in very tactical ways that disagree with other pieces of their narrative that we think are important. But in the U.S. far-right in particular, if you go down the list of the groups that were active in Charlottesville, they've all attended Russian conferences or been connected to Russian information architecture or received amplification from the Russian networks. I think that really points to a subject of interest from the Russian side that we need to be aware of. I and several of my colleagues, including Jim Ludes from Salve Regina University, were writing on Twitter about this after Charlottesville, and the bot attacks in response from both the Russian-crafted Bernie bots and the Russian-crafted far-right bots were intense and aggressive. So this is clearly something they don't really want discussed.

Mrs. SHAHEEN. Mr. Lansing, you talked about, in response to Congressman Smith's question about RT and Sputnik and efforts to address what they're doing in terms of presenting Russian propaganda, that you were concerned about retaliation. Do you believe that those two outlets are directly supported from Moscow, from Putin's government?

Mr. LANSING. Yes, I do.

Mrs. SHAHEEN. Do you, Ms. Hooper? Do you, Ms. McKew? [No audible response.]

And I have legislation that I introduced back earlier this year which would modernize our Foreign Agents Registration Act in a way that would give some teeth to the Justice Department, because it seems to me that they are dramatically exploiting a loophole. I would agree that under our system, they should be allowed to broadcast, but people need to understand what they're watching and that—because they claim that they are not directly connected to Putin's government and Moscow—Americans really are not as aware as we should be of what they represent. So that's really more of a statement than a question, but would you all support providing more teeth to FARA to allow us to close that loophole?

Ms. McKEW. As you know, Senator, I have been a foreign agent for different causes in the past, ones that I was happy to represent and fully disclosed and registered every contact and meeting and email to your office and others.

I do believe that right now FARA is basically voluntary. It was four, and now I think six, guys in one office. That's a good expansion. But there's a lot of belief that there are loopholes—there are really not—but it is not enforceable in its current form. There are some loopholes in the sense that think tanks aren't covered. There is foreign money that is being used to influence the Hill as well. That should be covered. There are lawyers who are happy to interpret for you how FARA does not apply. I do not have that lawyer, obviously, but others are happy to find them. And I think that, for that reason, the Justice Department needs to be clear about what the law actually says.

I think one particular point that needs to be more explicitly detailed—and I've had this conversation with many of my friends leaving government who I think have gotten the "don't worry, FARA doesn't apply to you" speech from others—if you read the statute the way I believe it was intended, if you are providing advice to a foreign government, political entity, state enterprise, et cetera on how to influence U.S. policy, even if you yourself are not making phone calls, sending emails, representing them actively in Congress or in the administration, you have to register. Many people don't. They sort of use this adviser label, claiming they have no responsibility. That, I think, really needs to be clarified and closed, because it's the space in which many people try to remain clean by not registering, but it is giving tremendous tools of influence to people who are willing to pay, because obviously most foreign interests are always going to encourage you not to register because, you know, who wants transparency?

Mrs. SHAHEEN. Sure, right.

Ms. McKEW. But the transparency point on RT and Sputnik, I think, is the right one. We do need to be careful about freedom of speech and information.

Mrs. SHAHEEN. Right.

Ms. McKEW. However, there should be disclaimers on the purpose of what this is.

Mrs. SHAHEEN. Absolutely. Do either of you want to comment?

Mr. LANSING. Sure. I will comment, Senator Shaheen. I'm not an expert on FARA. As a citizen, I would support the idea of strengthening FARA. As the CEO of the BBG, I would just make sure that you understand that there could be some reciprocal outcomes, depending on what happens as we strengthen FARA as it relates to Sputnik and RT.

Mrs. SHAHEEN. Sure.

Mr. LANSING. But that's just information for you to know.

And the last point I would make is the expression of what the networks of the BBG do around the world—Voice of America, Radio Free Europe—is really an expression of the value of free speech. And so I would put that into the mix as well, those two components, as you consider how to move forward.

Mrs. SHAHEEN. Well, thank you. I'm well aware of what the potential ramifications are. I've already been compared to McCarthy, my actions to McCarthyism. So——

Mr. LANSING. Hardly.

Mrs. SHAHEEN. Ms. Hooper.

Ms. HOOPER. I wanted to echo Mr. Lansing's concerns, that I know you're fully aware of. I think that it's important to perhaps not become too distracted by just RT and Sputnik.

Mrs. SHAHEEN. Absolutely.

Ms. HOOPER. I think in two ways, both in making FARA stronger, think about application across the board, what this is going to look like, and then in another way looking fully at other methods of influence and other influences on our media that is not just RT and Sputnik.

Mrs. SHAHEEN. Thank you. Well said.

Thank you, Mr. Chairman. And thank you very much for a really very informative and important hearing.

Mr. GARDNER. Thank you, Senator Shaheen.

And thanks to all of our colleagues on the Commission, the Helsinki Commission, who participated in today's hearing.

Thanks to the witnesses for your testimony, and I'm sure there will be follow up from a number of us on the Commission and with the Commission, work for additional questions, and I would ask you to respond as quickly as possible to anything on that front. But more than anything, grateful thanks to the Commission. And to everyone who participated in the hearing, thank you for attending. Thank you for listening online. I truly appreciate the participation.

And with that, this Helsinki Commission hearing is adjourned.

[Whereupon, at 11:31 a.m., the hearing ended.]

APPENDICES

PREPARED STATEMENT OF HON. CORY GARDNER, COMMISSIONER, COMMISSION ON SECURITY AND COOPERATION IN EUROPE

This hearing of the Helsinki Commission will come to order. Welcome, and good morning to everyone. I am honored to speak on behalf of Senator Wicker, the Commission's Chairman, and to preside over this hearing.

The Commission is mandated to monitor the compliance of participating states with consensus-based commitments of the OSCE. Today's hearing focuses on the pressing issue of Russian disinformation and how it undermines the security and human rights of people in the OSCE region.

Disinformation is an essential part of Russia's hybrid warfare against the United States and the liberal world order. As one of our distinguished panel witnesses today wrote in her recent article: "The Russian security state defines America as the primary adversary. The Russians know they cannot compete head-to-head with us—economically, militarily, technologically—so they create new battlefields. They are not aiming to become stronger than us, but to weaken us until we are equivalent."

Through its active measures campaign that includes aggressive interference in Western elections, Russia aims to sow fear, discord, and paralysis that undermines democratic institutions and weakens critical Western alliances, such as NATO and the EU.

Russia's ultimate goal is to replace the Western-led world order of laws and institutions with an authoritarian-led order that recognizes only masters and vassals. Our feeble response to Russian aggression in Ukraine and their interference in our elections has only emboldened the Kremlin to think that such a new world order is not only possible, but imminent.

We must not let Russian activities go with impunity. We must identify and combat them, utilizing every tool in our arsenal.

I am proud that my home state of Colorado is home to Fort Carson and the 10th Special Forces Group, an elite unit that has been at the tip of the spear in identifying and combating some of these malign Russian activities in European frontline states. I thank them for their important work, and for keeping our nation safe.

To help us lead our discussion today, I am pleased to introduce three distinguished witnesses.

Mr. John F. Lansing is the Chief Executive Officer and Director of the Broadcasting Board of Governors (BBG). He joined the BBG as CEO and Director in September 2015. Previously he was the President of Scripps Networks, where he is credited with guiding the company to become a leading developer of unique content across various media platforms.

Ms. Melissa Hooper is the current Director of Human Rights and Civil Society programs at Human Rights First. Ms. Hooper's research focuses on Russia's foreign policy strategies of spreading Russian influence and undermining democratic institutions in Eastern Europe, and how these strategies intersect with existing autocratic trends.

Ms. Molly McKew is an expert on information warfare and Russian disinformation policies. She currently heads an independent consulting firm, Fianna Strategies, advising governments and political parties on foreign policy and strategic communications. She has extensive regional experience, advising both Georgian and Moldovan governments. She also writes extensively on issues pertaining to Russian information warfare.

We will begin with Mr. Lansing who will offer his testimony and inform us what the BBG is doing to counter Russian disinformation in the OSCE region. We will then move onto to Ms. McKew's testimony where she will discuss information warfare and Russia's activity in this space. Finally, Ms. Hooper will present her analysis of Russian disinformation's influence over the German elections and its potential influence over future elections in Europe.

So, thank you to these distinguished members of today's expert panel for joining us today, and I look forward to our discussion as we strive to better understand this serious threat.

We may now begin with testimony by Mr. Lansing.

PREPARED STATEMENT OF HON. CHRISTOPHER H. SMITH, CO-CHAIMAN, COMMISSION ON SECURITY AND COOPERATION IN EUROPE

Thank you, Mr. Chairman, for leading our inquiry into Russian disinformation—a serious threat to democracy on both sides of the Atlantic

The most alarming thing about the Russian media's promotion of untruths and 'fake news' is the extent to which it is coordinated by the Russian government, and put in the service of a doctrine of war—the so-called "Gerasimov doctrine" of "hybrid war."

"Fake news" is far from unknown within our own society. We deal with it through freedom of speech, which allows it to be disproven, as well as through laws against libel and incitement.

Yet the case is totally different when a foreign government coordinates the production of "fake news" campaigns as part of hybrid war against us and our allies. I'd like to hear from our witnesses how they think our government can work with our allies to respond to the threat the Russian disinformation war poses against Ukraine, Lithuania, Latvia, Estonia, and Georgia. These are countries where disinformation is most fully put in service of "hybrid war."

How are we responding—and how should we? Most importantly, if Russian disinformation is hybrid war against these front-line allies, is our military and the NATO alliance making "counter-disinformation" part of a "hybrid defense" against this hybrid war?

Over the years, I've travelled to Russian many times on human rights missions—in the 1982 my first trip as a Congressman was to meet with Jewish 'refuseniks', in 1987 Frank Wolf and I visited Perm Camp 37 right before it closed. In the 1990s and early 2000s the meetings became friendlier, and I developed relationships with Russian legislators. Then came the Putin freeze. My last encounter with the Russian government came in February 2013. At that time, in response to congressional passage of the Magnitsky legislation denying U.S. visas to Russian officials responsible for the death of Sergei Magnitsky, the Russian government shut off all international adoptions to the U.S., including adoptions then already in the "pipeline." It was a heartless action. It punished Russian kids languishing in orphanages, preventing them from being united with loving families. Many of these kids had already established relationships with the adoptees.

At that time I requested a visa to travel to Russia to meet legislators, hoping to at least keep the adoptions that were already in process moving forward. I was an original cosponsor of the Magnitsky legislation and my request was denied—a State Department official told me that it was the first Russian visa denial to a U.S. Congressman in living memory. So I'm afraid that, being on a Russian visa-ban list, I don't have any recent experience in that country to bring to bear on our conversation. But the only other countries that have denied me visas are China and Cuba, two of the world's most repressive dictatorships. It's not a nice club to be in.

I look forward to our discussion today of this topic, so immediately relevant to the defense of some of our country's closest allies.

PREPARED STATEMENT OF HON. BENJAMIN CARDIN, RANKING
MEMBER, COMMISSION ON SECURITY AND COOPERATION IN EUROPE

Senator Gardner, thank you for presiding over this hearing today on behalf of Senator Wicker and discussing Russia and this most pressing and vital of concerns, Russian disinformation.

I have repeatedly stated that Russia is violating all of the Helsinki Final Act's Guiding Principles and now disinformation is the Russian State's latest strategy to undermine those guiding principles. Senator Gardner, I hope that today we can truly improve our understanding of the nature of Russian disinformation and the threat that it currently poses to the United States and other participating states of the OSCE.

In a world of rapid technological and social change and upheaval, Russia has not merely grasped the basic applications of new technology, but exploited it to introduce confusion and chaos in the media. This has culminated in the creation of the Gerasimov Doctrine, by Russian General Valery Gerasimov, which is the foundational document on the spread of disinformation and about which we will hear more today from one of our witnesses, Ms. Molly McKew.

As my colleague previously stated, we have seen the impact of this disinformation at home and abroad. Russian disinformation has spread throughout Ukraine, and especially impacted the Ukrainian state's response during the invasion of Crimea and the War in the Donbas. We have also seen the impact of Russian disinformation in the United States itself, with Russian Facebook users creating thousands of impersonation accounts and sharing pro-Kremlin information to the American public online during the 2016 election period.

This week—as the OSCE convenes Europe's largest annual human rights meeting in Warsaw, Poland—a long-time participant and leading voice in monitoring hate crimes, xenophobia and extremist violence in Russia is under threat. The SOVA Center is now being investigated as "undesirable." This is a painful reminder that Russia's "foreign agent law," used to target human rights groups and civil society in general, is one of Moscow's biggest global exports now, along with its disinformation.

I must note that this is the Helsinki Commission's third hearing on Russia this year. The Commission has investigated the extensive human rights abuses in Russia and the growing military threat that the Russian State poses. The scourge of disinformation is a serious and ongoing challenge Russia poses against the global community, in spite of its international treaties and commitments.

Senator Gardner, I hope that during this hearing we can grasp hold of how Russian disinformation threatens the United States and its allies; how well the United States is currently prepared to tackle this issue; and how capable we are, as a nation, to prevent and combat Russian disinformation in the future.

PREPARED STATEMENT OF HON. MICHAEL C. BURGESS, COMMISSIONER, COMMISSION ON SECURITY AND COOPERATION IN EUROPE

I want to thank the Chairman and Co-Chairman of the Helsinki Commission for convening this hearing today on such a timely and crucial topic.

Information warfare is the use of information, whether factual or false, to influence opinions, disrupt lines of communication, and undermine the values of a target for political advantage. This is exactly the behavior promulgated by the Russian government and its proxies during the 2016 Presidential election. Our intelligence community assessed that Vladimir Putin ordered an influence campaign aimed at the election in order to undermine faith in the democratic process by conducting covert intelligence operations and overtly disseminate false information.

Russia's attempt to influence our election was not the only goal; Russia is conducting a long-term campaign to undermine the U.S.-led liberal democratic order. Previously, Russia conducted campaigns against Estonia, Georgia, and Ukraine. In addition to disinformation efforts in the U.S., Russia is aiming to disrupt the European Union and sow distrust of NATO to accelerate its dissolution.

Today, Russia begins a weeklong series of military drills known as Zapad, or West, with Belarus that will place thousands of troops along the border with the Baltic States and Poland. This exercise is expected to be much bigger than previous iterations. While Russia insists Zapad poses no threat, it is clearly part of Vladimir Putin's strategy to expand Russia's sphere of influence and increase military capacity along NATO borders. In response, the United States sent 600 American paratroopers to the area for the duration of the exercise.

In 2009, President Obama reversed a plan to build missile interceptors and a radar station in Poland. As a result, Russia is no longer deterred from aggressive behavior on NATO's periphery. The strength of NATO, largely based on U.S. backing, is a direct threat to Russia and Vladimir Putin's strategy of expansion. We must be prepared to respond to this threatening activity.

Executing Russia's long-term expansion strategy is much easier when the countries and institutions that can prevent Russian expansion may be fighting a disinformation campaign at home. Unfortunately, Russia has perfected the control of information by first imposing strict limits on its citizens. This problem is two-fold; it allows Russia to control what its citizens know about their own country, and it prevents Russian citizens from learning the truth about foreign government actions, particularly from the United States. This is why many Russians are reported to blame the United States for hardships resulting from sanctions rather than blaming the Russian government for behaving in a way that incurs sanctions in the first place.

This type of censorship is absent in the United States because we support freedom of speech and the pursuit of knowledge. Our citizens have always trusted our news organizations to report what is going on in our country and around the world. When reporting is undermined by false information, it is difficult to determine what is real because the news becomes a game of "he said, she said," or rather "he reported, she reported." How are our citizens to know what is accurate and what is false?

There is no evidence that Russian interference in our election amounted to the actual changing of votes. With the German election coming up in a couple of weeks, we must continue to fight Russia's attempt to meddle in foreign elections and threaten our NATO allies. It is paramount that the United States engages with the American public and our allies to ensure that Russia's information war does not succeed.

PREPARED STATEMENT OF JOHN LANSING, CHIEF EXECUTIVE OFFICER AND DIRECTOR, BROADCASTING BOARD OF GOVERNORS (BBG)

Senator Gardner, Co-Chair Smith, Ranking Member Cardin, and Members of the Commission, thank you for inviting me to speak today about the Broadcasting Board of Governors' (BBG) and U.S. International Media efforts to counter Russian propaganda and disinformation.

Background

I currently serve as the Chief Executive Officer and Director of BBG, where I oversee all operational aspects of U.S. international media comprising five networks:

The Voice of America, Office of Cuba Broadcasting (Radio and TV Marti), Radio Free Asia, Radio Free Europe/Radio Liberty, and the Middle East Broadcasting Networks including Alhurra TV and Radio Sawa.

As U.S. international media, the BBG's mission is to inform, engage, and connect people around the world in support of freedom and democracy. We produce news on all media platforms including radio, television, online, and mobile digital and social media. Collectively, our programs reach 278 million people on a weekly basis in more than 100 countries and 61 languages. According to Gallup data, our audience increased by 52 million from 2015. The fastest growing segment of that audience is our newly expanded commitment to digital distribution which helps us target younger future leaders.

The BBG provides consistently accurate and compelling journalism that opens minds and stimulates debate. We demonstrate values that reflect our society: **freedom, openness, democracy, and hope**.

This advances U.S. national interests by fostering societies that enjoy greater stability and prosperity, live in peace with their neighbors, value universal human rights and reject terrorism and extremism. Such societies make better political allies and trade partners for the United States.

This mission, granted by Congress at the end of World War II, remains vitally important. During World War II, the Voice of America fought against Nazi propaganda and the absence of information by beaming accurate and unbiased news and information into shuttered societies. RFE/RL was founded during the Cold War to break through the Kremlin's wall of tightly controlled media in the Soviet Union and in Eastern Europe with truthful professional journalism and by documenting the anti-Soviet sentiment of the citizens under the authoritarian regime.

Current Media Environment

Today we are encountering a global explosion of disinformation, propaganda and lies fed by multiple authoritarian regimes and non-state actors like ISIS, as they deploy digital media and social media platforms to target vulnerable citizens with false narratives. House Foreign Affairs Chairman Ed Royce, referring to Russian propaganda specifically, terms it ***the weaponization of informa-***

tion," and I believe that captures the severity of the negative impact quite well.

From Russia and its periphery, to China and East Asia, Iran and the Middle East, to Cuba, Venezuela and large parts of Latin America—audiences are under a disinformation assault from authoritarian regimes and are desperate for credible information. The five U.S. International Media Networks of the BBG fill that void.

To meet the challenge head-on, all five BBG networks are rapidly expanding our traditional radio and television distribution to digital, mobile and social networks so we are on the same playing field as our adversaries.

Importantly, over 80 percent of our weekly audience on all platforms considers our content to be trustworthy, based on data compiled by Gallup, and we highly value the trust our audience has placed in us.

At the same time, global press freedom is at its lowest point in over a decade. According to the 2017 Freedom House report on Freedom of the Press, only 13 percent of the world's population live in countries with a fully free press. Of the ten worst offenders— which include Cuba, Iran, North Korea and Syria—all are covered by one or more of the BBG's networks. In each of these countries, BBG networks challenge limitations on the press and provide alternative sources of news against state- or extremist-sponsored accounts.

Russian Actions

In Russia, the Kremlin propaganda machine is breathing new life into a strategy of *dezinformatsiya*, or disinformation, operations to influence opinions about the United States and its allies and partners. Essentially, it's the weaponization of information that Chairman Royce describes. For example, Russian disinformation campaigns claim that the United States is covertly testing chemical warfare in Ukraine and that the U.S. has more than 400 laboratories around the world for biological weapons.

State-sponsored broadcasters such as Russia Today (RT) and Sputnik are expanding their global operations, opening new bureaus and developing new programming. Earlier this year in Washington, DC, a Bluegrass radio station sponsored by NPR on 105.5 FM was replaced by Sputnik radio offering listeners the Kremlin spin on U.S. news and politics. Outside these organizations, Twitter trolls and social media bots magnify the Kremlin-supported message.

Unlike Cold War propaganda, Russian disinformation campaigns do not seek to sway listeners to the Russian point of view; rather they strive to undermine the notion of objective truth and foster social divisions—delegitimizing Western democracies while drawing negative attention away from Russia.

In essence the Russian strategy is to destroy the very idea of an objective, verifiable set of facts. In their world the death of facts is the first step towards creating the alternative reality that helps them gain and keep authority with no accountability. If everything is a lie, then the biggest liar wins. That is what we are up against.

BBG Response

While the threat is not new, the battlespace is changing, and the BBG is adapting to meet this challenge head on. We are one part of the overall government effort taking a global approach to countering Russian disinformation across a variety of platforms. I'd like to detail some of these key initiatives:

1) Current Time

Since Russian aggression against Crimea and eastern Ukraine started in early 2014, BBG language services at VOA and RFE/RL have added or expanded more than 35 new programs in Russian and other languages of the former Soviet space. The flagship of this effort is a 24/7 television and digital news network that BBG launched in February 2017 called *Current Time* , or *"Nastoyashchee Vremya."* In Russian, the name has a double meaning: "right now" or the current time; and "the real deal," which plays off the name of Russia's traditional nightly newscast *"Vremya,"* meaning "time."

The *Current Time* mission is to provide a constant stream of accurate, professional, independent, unbiased news to Russian speakers in Russia, the Russian periphery, and around the world including major capitals such as Berlin, Jerusalem, and London. For example, in Stockholm or Istanbul, Russian travelers may turn on the television in their hotel room to find *Current Time* next to CNN on the channel list.

Produced by RFE/RL in a first-ever, unique partnership with VOA—another BBG network— *Current Time* represents the next generation of digital news for BBG. Viewers access programming throughout the region on the *Current Time* website. Individual *Current Time* programs play on 39 affiliates in 14 countries, but the full 24/7 channel is distributed to over 23 countries on 59 satellite, cable, and digital distributors. The network also develops social media videos and other content, expanding the reach of *Current Time* and offering alternative sources of information in a Kremlin-controlled environment.

The level of access to *Current Time* programming varies. In Russia, *Current Time* TV and radio broadcasts are not permitted on domestic television and radio airwaves, but audience members can access content through the website and YouTube. In Lithuania—a key Kremlin propaganda target and currently *Current Time* 's largest market—programming airs on two public broadcasting stations and is viewed by 8.2 percent of the adult population each week. Additionally, the BBG is finalizing negotiations with Lithuania Radio & Television to place *Current Time* on their nationwide Terrestrial Digital TV system—with signals covering 98 percent of the Lithuanian population and reaching into Belarus, Poland, and Kaliningrad.

The *Current Time* network produces daily news shows on the United States and global events. It also features reports on business, entrepreneurship, civil society, culture, and corruption. Because *Current Time* is its own branded network on its own platform, BBG also has the flexibility to interrupt programming to bring late-breaking news and analysis or unfiltered, simultaneously translated broadcasting of major events. For example, during the 2016 U.S. election, VOA and RFE/RL provided a 5-hour marathon of live television programming with reports from around the country and live results and analysis.

Digital statistics—such as the number of video views, comments, and shares—indicate that the *Current Time* network is yielding results online. From January to July 2017, *Current Time* social videos were viewed more than 300 million times on various digital platforms—nearly three times the number of views during the same period in 2016. Half of these views came from Russia. Further, in May alone, *Current Time* achieved a record 40 million video views across social media platforms. This impressive start is just the beginning, and as time goes on, we will have the opportunity to add to this digital data through our traditional media surveys that measure both reach and influence.

2) Targeting the Russian periphery

Current Time is only the latest BBG effort in the Russian periphery and Eastern Europe. VOA and RFE/RL programming in Russia and the Russian periphery targets audiences in 23 media markets and is consumed by over 24 million adults on a weekly basis in 20 languages. In Kosovo and Albania, over 60 percent of the adult population tunes in on a weekly basis.

3) Meeting Russia on a global stage

If we discuss the Russian disinformation campaign only in terms of Russian language efforts, we are missing the global context of what is truly a world-wide campaign. Russian-sponsored programming is available in Latin America, Africa, the Middle East, and across Europe in Arabic, Spanish, French, English, and other languages.

In Latin America, for example, VOA has strong relationships with hundreds of TV and radio affiliates. Every day our reporters offer live VOA feeds from DC into local news programs in Mexico, Colombia, Venezuela and other countries. They cover and explain developments in the United States and U.S. foreign policy and also develop special programs in partnership with local stations. For example, in Nicaragua, VOA and local partners are developing a series on the Russian presence in that country.

If VOA content were no longer available, Russian media and other state-sponsored broadcasters (including China's CCTV and Iran's HispanTV) would be more than willing to provide their own slanted content replacing the VOA. Some affiliates have reported that they have been offered payment to air programming, which VOA does not provide in that region. Instead, VOA offers cogent programming and a brand trusted by Latin American audiences.

We have also deployed a new brand called *Polygraph*, a joint RFE/RL and VOA website in English to call out Russian lies and educate global audiences on media literacy and how to spot fake news. Within the next few weeks, BBG will launch a Russian language version of this website.

Russia has jumped to criticize these and other BBG efforts. On *Current Time* and other content aimed at the Russian periphery, a Russian state news organization charged that these programs are all produced by "Russian people who put the interests of America above the interests of Russia." Our journalists have also come under attack. For example, RFE/RL contributor Mykola Semena was indicted on criminal charges in Crimea for so-called separatist activities, or rather professional journalism and telling the truth. His most recent hearing occurred on August 31. We take the safety and security our journalists very seriously, and believe that this and other incidents demonstrate the Kremlin is clearly irritated by our efforts.

BBG Challenges

With the support of Congress and the generosity of the American taxpayers, BBG's budget has expanded over the last few years.

In addition to nearly half-billion-dollar combined budgets of RT, Sputnik, and other Russian international media, the Russian government also targets Russian speakers around the world with the vast resources of its domestic state-controlled news and entertainment networks.

The BBG's mission is to broadcast internationally; thus, BBG is constrained by law from programming in the United States, although we are now allowed to share content with U.S. media outlets upon their request. RT, Sputnik and others are free to broadcast in the U.S.—because the U.S. values free speech and freedom of the press, and we extend those rights to all. Russian speakers in the United States are free to choose not only from RT and Sputnik, but from dozens of Russian language stations whose scope is the equivalent of CNN, Fox, CBS, ABC, NBC, Bloomberg and other entertainment channels. We would welcome access to the Russian market to allow our networks to broadcast freely there in the spirit of reciprocity.

Make no mistake—the United States is facing information warfare, and I don't use that term lightly. The BBG is an essential element of the national security response. The export of U.S. journalism and the values of free media and free speech speak to the world as much as U.S. boots on the ground. Like defense, development, and diplomacy, U.S. international media—accurate, balanced and true—is an essential part of our standing on the world stage.

I'll close with a quote from Edward R. Murrow, former director of the U.S. Information Agency and a much-respected journalist of the 20th Century, when he testified before Congress in 1963:

> To be persuasive we must be believable;
>
> to be believable we must be credible;
>
> to be credible we must be truthful.

His words ring true today, more than ever.
Thank you.

PREPARED STATEMENT OF MOLLY M. MCKEW, CEO, FIANNA STRATEGIES

I am grateful for the opportunity to share some of my experiences countering Russian information warfare. I've spent the past decade watching the deployment of Russian information operations across the European frontier, including in Georgia, Moldova, Ukraine, and the Baltic states. I have done this primarily as a partisan, working for political actors and other groups being attacked by these Russian initiatives, so I tend to come at this from a different perspective than others. Russia is constantly acting, assessing, and refining their information capabilities, which have become an embedded and normalized part of our information landscape. We must be clear about what these measures aim to achieve and their impact, and bring a renewed sense of urgency to defending our nation.

OVERVIEW OF RUSSIA'S INFORMATION WAR AGAINST WESTERN SOCIETIES

It is essential that we evaluate the challenge of 'Russian propaganda' from the right perspective in order to develop effective counter measures.

First, disinformation is a means of warfare. It is the core component of a war being waged by the Russian state against the West, and against the United States in particular.

Second, the primary line of effort in this war is conducted in English. We have failed to secure our information space, allowing our self-defined 'primary adversary' to shape and in some cases control it at will, often blind to what they aim to achieve. This provides the Kremlin a significant strategic advantage.

Third, we have only just begun to understand the scope and scale of resources, formal and informal, that Russia devotes to information warfare—which means we have failed to understand the importance the Kremlin ascribes to these efforts. Some resources are devoted to forms we know—RT, Sputnik, etc—and others to forms we are coming to know—automated actors like botnets, and amplifiers like trolls—but far more of these measures are still deep within the shadow space, acting along parallel lines of effort.

It bears repeating: it's not propaganda; it's information warfare. It is, in many respects, the war that matters most. In our strategic thinking, information operations of this kind are meant to amplify military operations. In Russian doctrine, it is the other way around: military operations amplify information operations. The 'smoke and mirrors' are a primary means of power projection.

The information warfare being used against us aims to erode political will, in ourselves and our allies, to defend what defines us; to sow doubt and division, discord and chaos, in order to reshape an environment where American power is less effective; to target the minds of our soldiers and leaders, activists and influencers, voters and citizens, using subversive means; to spark political unrest, and make us question that democracy can provide just, free, equitable, secure, and prosperous societies.

And it is working.

We have seen this type of information warfare deployed against other nations. There is ample evidence of the extent to which Russia will go to shape demographics, politics, and social structures in its near abroad, using military, economic, political, and cultural coercion. But we, as Americans, want to believe it doesn't work on us—that oceans are still a barrier to foreign invasion, that we are immune to these manipulations, particularly from an opponent far weaker, militarily and economically.

In their weakness, the Kremlin bets big. So far, the gamble has paid off—because for years they have been strolling across an open battlefield.

To secure our information space, we need an integrated understanding of the threat, and an integrated set of measures that can be taken to counter it, including:

- *Enhanced clarity of the threat and its impact:* We must clearly identify the tools and tactics being used against us in the information space, and effective means of disrupting them.
- *Whole-of-government response:* We need unity of mission to secure the American information space, including organizing our diplomatic, military, and intelligence assets to counter information warfare via a whole-of-government approach. Nongovernmental assets and actors also play a vital part in any effective response, and should be creatively engaged.
- *Rethinking authorities:* We must reevaluate the role of US military/counterintelligence actors in securing our information space during this time of rapidly escalating threats. Our most experienced assets should not be boxed-out of defending the American people.
- *Develop rapid response capability for irregular information warfare:* Build capacity to execute local rapid information operations (positive and interceptive) manned by sanctioned irregulars (US Special Forces and counterintelligence assets, plus independent actors).
- *Give Americans defensive tools:* This occurs via three strands. First, speaking clearly to the public about the threat. Second, developing practices for enhancing national 'cognitive resistance,' particularly in groups being targeted by Russian operations. Third, building stronger data/privacy protections for Americans to limit the coercive applications of 'big data.'
- *Motivate/activate the American populace:* We need political leaders with the will to speak clearly to our people about our principles and values—the narratives and truths that matter.
- *Whole-of-alliance approach to securing the information space:* A better-coordinated US response mechanism will be better positioned to collaborate with and lead our NATO/EU allies in countering Russian information operations. A range of different mechanisms have been developed by certain European military, government, and civil society actors that would be greatly enhanced by clear strategic goals and supporting resources.
- *Social media evaluation/regulation:* Adversarial forces are using social media platforms to attack our societies. We need to consider applying rules to how paid and automated content can be spread through social media. This is not about limiting

the free flow of information and ideas—we should never seek to emulate Russian control tactics or the means used by other authoritarian states—but restricting the ability for coercive targeting and the simulation of human supporters/movements to promote coercive propaganda.

- *Enhanced understanding of aims of Russian financial flows:* Russian disinformation has purpose. So does the export of its capital. We must be far more aware of the aims of this financial flow, especially investments into/partnerships with American technology companies.

These measures will be discussed further in the final section.

There is an urgent need for effective counter measures. Russian efforts fuel conflict and chaos in Europe, the Middle East, Afghanistan, Asia, and the Arctic. While our attention is elsewhere, spread thin across crises and putting out fires, the other tools in Russia's guerrilla arsenal have time to gain vantage. This arsenal is backed by considerable state financial resources. We have a tendency to see Russian kleptocracy as a means of buying super-yachts and penthouses. It isn't. It's about buying us. The range of tools this money supports is unnerving in its informality, depth, and potential.

Russia's war in Syria has been a giant arms expo meant to demo and sell a new generation of Russian weaponry. The Russian information control model is just as much on display and in demand. President Putin recently discussed the opportunities and perils of artificial intelligence, adding: "We will certainly share our technology with the rest of the world, the way we are doing now with atomic and nuclear technology." [1] We have every interest in preventing the proliferation of effective tools and models of computational propaganda. [2]

Ten years since a cyber attack on Estonia, nine years after Russia's invasion of Georgia, almost four years since the invasion of Ukraine, ten months since we got a red alert on the information war being waged against the American people—and our actions says we're still trying to decide if this is a threat that we need to take seriously. For example: Congress mandated the creation of the State Department's Global Engagement Center to help counter Russian disinformation, authorizing considerable financial resources to the cause. These resources have neither been allocated nor spent. [3] Other efforts have directed resources to countering Russian narrative—in Russian. [4] Very little has been done about the English language disinformation targeting Americans.

Russia has corrupted our information space through countless means. Right now, there are efforts to analyze the war; expose the

---

[1] Putin's remarks can be read here in English: https://sputniknews.com/russia/201709011057000758-p 1 utin-schoolchildren- world-lord/

[2] *Computational propaganda is the use of automation—including tools like botnets and artificial intelligence (AI), directed by algorithms and the harvesting of data to create targeting profiles—to influence opinion via the internet and social media.*

[3] Toosi, Nahal. "Tillerson spurns $80 million to counter ISIS, Russian propaganda." *Politico.* Aug 2, 2017. http:// www.politico.com/story/2017/08/02/tillerson-isis-russia-propaganda-241218 Toosi, Nahal. "Tillerson moves toward accepting funding for fighting Russian propaganda." *Politico.* Aug 31, 2017. http://www.politico.com/story/2017/08/31/rex-tillerson-funding-russian-propaganda-242224

[4] CBS News. "U.S. launches TV network as alternative to Russian propaganda." Feb 9, 2017. https://www.cbsnews.-com/news/us-current-time-tv-network-rfe-russia-russian-propaganda-misinformation-rt/

war; map the war—but very little is being done to *fight* the war, or to provide resources, mandate, or authorities to those with the skill sets to do so. While we investigate and analyze and discuss, the diverse initiatives underway from the Kremlin have accelerated in Europe, across the globe, and in the United States.

UNDERSTANDING THE AIMS OF RUSSIAN INFORMATION WARFARE: EXAMPLES FROM THE FIELD

Information tools are the new superweapons—like chemical weapons in WWI or the atomic bomb in WWII, they shift the fundamental balance of power and fear. In their essence, Russian measures aim for the complete domination of an information landscape in order to influence the minds of a population. These measures target, in particular, military personnel, political leaders, and vulnerable, disenfranchised, and unmoored elements of society—but they also target society writ large by focusing on identity, historical memory, topics of a divisive nature, and more. These measures aim to harden specific aspects of identity; to radicalize elements of society; and to build the activation potential of a population.

Disinformation can be lies or partial truth. What matters is that it has purpose. It is targeted against specific parts of a population using crafted narrative, and it aims to mobilize groups of people to act in specific ways. So this is not about words, but about achieving concrete results. Ideas lead to decisions; once a decision is made, it will be rationalized, entrenching the idea.

The technological tools of producing, disseminating, and amplifying disinformation matter—but far less than the construction of that information to be persuasive and coercive against the audience. In this regard, two things matter: narrative and storytelling. *Narrative* is the overarching construct of the information, providing answers to questions of who we are and why things are the way they are. *Storytelling* is how you build and transmit narrative.

"What did it aim to achieve?" is a more important question in evaluating disinformation than what is true. Fighting it must also have a purpose. If we aren't clear what that purpose is—what we are fighting for, what we believe—then we can't win. Russia goes to great pains to downplay their role in information operations because exposing them can restrict their freedom of movement. Some of the most effective Russian disinformation aims to make you believe Russia is weak and disorganized, and the Kremlin excels at finding local actors to act as masks and passthroughs. There can be many different lines of effort aiming to achieve different outcomes in different audiences. But there is a pattern and a texture to how these efforts form and coalesce, to the narrative they use, and to the results they can yield. Below are a few examples from my own experiences.

Shaping the Baltic information environment: During the past year, I worked as the strategic director of a project to enhance Baltic Russian-language media. This was a modest initiative, primarily small grants to journalists and producers. Nonetheless, I can document about six attempts by Kremlin-connected actors to gain access to the project and our work. This illustrates how deeply dominance in the Baltic information environment is a preeminent concern of Russian efforts.

In the Baltic states, there is a basic three-pronged approach: rewriting history, demonizing NATO, and sewing doubt about the efficacy of pro-Western governing forces. Understanding the narrative of these operations is critical: efforts to demonize occupation-era Baltic resistance movements or deny the existence of a pact between Stalin and Hitler sometimes seem obscure to us, for example, but the purpose is to create justification for modern Russian state actions and ambitions. These nations are inundated with Russian and English language content generated by the Russians as they aim to shape the perception of specific groups. Russia also shapes the external narrative on the Baltics by providing English language news from the region. A recent report found that computational propaganda plays a significant role here: a quarter of the accounts posting in English on Twitter in the Baltics and Poland were likely bots/ automated, responsible for 46% of the total English language content on NATO. [5]

Moldovan identity politics: Unlike the Baltic states, Moldova does not have a strong national identity and is quite divided as a society. It also has a terrible information environment, with most of the national media controlled by the nominally pro-Western oligarch whose party has captured most of the governmental institutions. This is fertile ground for propaganda and information operations, particularly nasty personal attacks—but the way information moves and is used helps to expose agendas, in many respects. In the last presidential election, for example, which was won by the pro-Russian candidate, the media holdings of the 'pro-Western' oligarch mentioned above amplified Russian attacks and disinformation against the pro- European candidate in the race. [6]

In Moldova, false information is also frequently introduced via Russian information channels to create positive sentiments about the unpopular ruling force—a phenomenon we called 'double disinfo,' disinformation meant to make another piece of untrue information believable. A recent example of this had pro-Russian social media accounts leak a fake letter in which USAID complained to the ruling party that they were not doing enough to fight Russian information in Moldova. [7] When the letter was exposed as a fake, the false counter-positive—that the ruling party was fighting Russian information—is made more believable.

Voter mobilization/suppression in Georgia: Georgia's parliamentary elections in 2012, during which I worked as an advisor to the Georgian National Security Council, were the first where I saw Russian-connected political forces looking to hire Western firms who could teach them about micro-targeting and other social media-based information tools. American teams marketing themselves as

---

[5] NATO Stratcom COE. *Robotrolling* 2017/1. http://stratcomcoe.org/robotrolling-20171

[6] Jamestown Foundation. "Moldova's De Facto Ruler Enthrones Pro-Russia President." *Eurasia Daily Monitor Volume: 13 Issue: 196.* December 14 2016. https://www.ecoi.net/local__link/333654/461950__en.html Vlas, Cristian. "Old Fashioned Skulduggery Overshadows Elections in Moldova." Emerging Europe. Nov 19, 2016. http://emerging-europe.com/voices/voices-intl-relations/old-fashioned-skulduggery-overshadows-the-elections-inmoldova/

[7] The source of the letter was: https://twitter.com/Urugvayintellig/status/904633014541574144/photo/1

contributors to the Obama victory were hired by Bidzina Ivanishvili to operationalize black information campaigns, which contributed to getting tens of thousands of people in the streets before the election. Most of what was happening in the social media landscape was completely opaque to the ruling party until well after the election: the messaging was designed not to touch anyone who was a consistent supporter of the government.

One aspect of this overall campaign that I would highlight as a favored Russian tactic: the use of diversion. The online media campaigns cultivated an intense environment of fear of the potential for violence—rumors that the government would declare martial law instead of holding the vote; claims Russia would invade again if the ruling party won; threats of disruption and violence at the polls. This consumed the attention of the government/ruling party and the diplomatic/observer community. But this was always meant to be a distraction from real lines of effort: black media campaigns and traditional voter mobilization efforts. I mention this because I believe there was a similar Russian diversion effort during the US elections: US intelligence and the Obama White House feared disruption of our elections via the hacking of electoral and voting infrastructure, and significantly less attention was paid to the information operations being run. In both cases, the lesson we should learn: information operations are a primary line of effort from the Kremlin.

Narrative themes during elections/referenda: While every now and then there is a Marine Le Pen—an openly pro-Kremlin political candidate—arguably the more dangerous new archetype of candidates favored by the Kremlin are those who amplify Kremlin narrative as part of their political platforms without being so openly pro-Russian. These themes can include: nationalism/anti-globalism/anti-integration; anti-refugee/anti-immigration; 'traditional' identity and values; anti-tolerance, especially anti-LGBT sentiments; to name a few. Knowingly or not, parties focusing on these themes contribute to achieving core goals important to the Kremlin—rejecting Western liberal democracy; weakening NATO, the EU, and the transatlantic alliance; deepening divides inside our alliances and our nations that can be exploited. This model is critical in many countries, especially some former captive Soviet nations, where pro-Russian political forces would be unable to gain significant following. But the governing agendas of these parties tend to be more inward looking and de facto downplay the significance of the existential threat from Russia, on which the basic line tends to be: "Wouldn't it be nice if we had a better relationship with Russia (especially economically)?"

The degree to which Russia exploits this ideological space, sometimes very tactically, should not be underrated. Some groups knowingly engage the Kremlin for resources and support, glad to have an ally; others may receive support via amplification in Russian information architecture, whether they asked for it or not. Anti-LGBT sentiment has been a vital avenue for the Kremlin to cultivate a new generation of political and cultural allies across Europe and the United States. In elections across Europe in the past two years, anti-refugee and anti-migrant sentiment has been used repeatedly to galvanize nationalistic voters; this has been a core theme deployed in the German elections which will be held later this month, as it was used before in France and the Netherlands and the Brexit referendum. Just this week, we have news that Russian accounts on Facebook were used to organize anti-immigrant rallies in the US during our election. [8] There are dozens of examples that could be given, but that one makes it the most clear: this isn't just information but the hope to elicit behavioral change.

ASSESSING THE STATE OF CONFLICT AND READINESS IN THE INFORMATION WAR

In order to propose defensive and offensive information warfare strategies, it helps to define the current doctrinal and strategic landscape clearly. This starts with the 'Gerasimov Doctrine.' The Gerasimov Doctrine builds a framework for the use of non-military tactics, including information warfare, that are not auxiliary to the use of force but the preferred way to conduct war. Chaos is the strategy the Kremlin pursues, aiming to achieve an environment of permanent unrest and conflict within enemy states and alliances where a weak Russian state can exert outsize influence and control. [9] But we've been talking about the Gerasimov Doctrine like it's the holy grail of understanding Russia since 2013. We reanalyze it over and over. Meanwhile Russian doctrine has evolved further, articulating how to apply these core concepts across multiple strands of warfare.

> *In the 21st century we have seen a tendency toward blurring the lines between the states of war and peace. The very "rules of war" have changed. The role of nonmilitary means of achieving political and strategic goals has grown, and, in many cases, they have exceeded the power of force of weapons in their effectiveness. All this is supplemented by military means of a concealed character.The information space opens wide asymmetrical possibilities for reducing the fighting potential of the enemy. Among such actions are the use of special-operations forces and internal opposition to create a permanently operating front through the entire territory of the enemy state, as well as informational actions, devices, and means that are constantly being perfected.*

> *The Value of Science is in the Foresight—*
> Gen. Valery Gerasimov, Russian Chief of the General Staff, Feb 2013

> *The military strategies applied by the leading nations stipulate that dominance in information space is essential in*

---

[8] Collins, Ben, Kevin Poulsen, Spencer Ackerman. "Russia Used Facebook Events to Organize Anti-Immigrant Rallies on U.S. Soil." *The Daily Beast.* Sept 11, 2017. http://www.thedailybeast.com/exclusive-russia-used-facebook-eventsto- organize-anti-immigrant-rallies-on-us-soil

[9] McKew, Molly. "The Gerasimov Doctrine." *Politico Magazine.* Sept/Oct 2017 ed. http://www.politico.com/magazine/ story/2017/09/05/gerasimov-doctrine-russia-foreign-policy-215538 McKew, Molly. "Putin's Real Long Game." *Politico Magazine.* Jan 1, 2017. http://www.politico.com/magazine/story/ 2017/01/putins-real-long-game-214589

warfare. This task requires engagement of media and social networks. They are complemented by information, psychological, and technical influence.. The [Russian] Armed Forces are currently gaining their combat experience in Syria. They have a unique opportunity to test modern weapons and military equipment in adverse climate conditions. It is necessary to continue this military practice in the Syrian campaign and draw the lessons to adapt and improve Russian weapons. It should be noted that victory depends not only on the material but also the spiritual resources—the nation's cohesion and desire to confront the aggressor at all cost.

The World on the Verge of War—Gerasimov, March 2017

The evidence points to new types of military action in upcoming conflicts. Our 20 years of experience insist on the importance of irregular forces (guerrillas). They are integrated into military personnel and excel at combat endurance. Furthermore, irregular operations achieve the most political goals of war. If guerrilla forces fail, defeat is imminent, regardless of conventional and special forces superiority. Guerrillas are capable of large-scale operations and consistent military action pursuing tactical and strategic goals. Coordination with guerrillas is always complicated. Nonetheless, their actions must be coordinated with the regular armed forces, in particular during special operations. In other words, WWIII guerrillas must be under the authority of a single commander. Thus, these unique forces are vital for the Russian Armed Forces.. If provided with the information and intelligence available to the regular armed forces, even small numbers of irregular troops can produce immediate results.

The Guerrilla Payees—Konstantin Sivkov, retired General Staff officer, April 2017

What we see in these excerpts:[10] Russia is operationalizing a fundamentally guerrilla approach to total warfare in order to achieve strategic political objectives—a global imperialist insurgency.

Both the United States and Russia, for different reasons, have made the determination that fighting and defending against unconventional warfare is the key to future war. But we pursue it differently. The US has shifted toward special operators and the use of drones; training partner nations, and helping them conduct strikes on targets; running defensive information operations; bolstering our efforts with civilian-military affairs projects. Russia does everything else. The nature of their efforts is not defensive or retaliatory, but entirely offensive.

The Kremlin is recruiting people, groups, and societies into a dirty war.

---

[10] *The Value of Science is in the Foresight*—https://inmoscowsshadows.wordpress.com/2014/07/06/the-gerasimovdoctrine- and-russian-non-linear-war/; *The World on the Verge of War*—http://vpk-news.ru/articles/35591; *The Guerrilla Payees*—http://vpk-news.ru/articles/36159

SECURING OUR INFORMATION SPACE IS ABOUT ENGLISH LANGUAGE INFORMATION, NOT RUSSIAN

When we speak of 'Russian propaganda,' we don't really mean Russian *language* propaganda as much as we mean Russian state efforts to export disinformation into local languages in many European countries, and into English in particular, which have drastically accelerated since 2013. Russia invests heavily in media resources; learning, creating, and adapting tools for targeting information to specific individuals; and automating disinformation across social media platforms in ways to reach specific people, counter/promote specific ideas, and game algorithms to give primacy to the Russian version of 'truth.' In many respects, our entire information space has been corrupted by or made vulnerable to Russian information operations. The Russian language space, in comparison, is controlled, insular and collapsing on itself without captive nations—as the chairman of the Duma Committee on Education and Science recently noted, while railing against the 'linguistic hegemony of English,' the number of Russian speakers has declined by 50 million people since 1991. [11]

But the 'linguistic hegemony of English' also makes us vulnerable. Disinformation is more powerful in English because English is the language of the internet. It's a bigger echo chamber, and it gives more reach to target audiences vulnerable to core parts of Russian narrative. The US also has incredibly weak data/privacy protections, thus enabling the harvesting and analysis of data for cognitive targeting in ways that should make us profoundly uncomfortable.

Looking at information warfare as a map exercise: Russia has used disinformation to project the line of conflict forward, further from their borders—to effectively erase borders while creating the virtual 'buffer zone' they can't have territorially. Our immediate response should seek to mirror this—not by addressing a problem hundreds of miles behind the line of conflict (Russian language) but by moving the line of conflict further from our country, back toward the aggressor. If this war has no borders, it is a fluid space that we must constantly expand and enhance not to lose. In real terms, there is no 'defending' the information space. The only defense is offense—illuminating and educating people on the threat, and promoting our principles and values.

Russia likes to position all their doctrine as a 'response' to Western actions. A more helpful way to gain insight into what the Kremlin believes they can achieve with unconventional warfare, and with information warfare in particular, is to understand that all the tools they deploy against us, they used against the Russian people first. We need to secure our information space, just as we would any other border. The Russians did this to their own information space before invading ours—building parallel social media, controlling access to content, flooding the local media landscape with free entertainment content, shutting down most of the inde-

---

[11] The remarks can be read here in English: https://themoscowtimes.com/news/russian-language-losing-out-of-english- hegemony-says-official-58779

pendent media, now using automated social media content to amplify and bury specific views.

AN INTEGRATED STRATEGY FOR SECURING OUR INFORMATION SPACE

There are four key groups for crafting an effective response to Russian information operations: *government* (including military, intelligence, etc); *industry* (tech and data companies); *civil society*; and *citizenry*. Government plays an essential coordination role.

These are complicated issues, touching on freedom of speech and expression, national security, and more. We cannot use the same means of information control as the Kremlin to secure our information space. Our mirror-world version of Russian information control: not to control the internal information environment, but ensure its integrity; not to harden views, but to develop positive cognitive resistance efforts to build resilience in our population; not to argue that there 'is no truth,' but to promote the values and idea that we know matter.

Securing our information space has less to do with cybersecurity than building resilience in our citizenry, and re-crafting the ways that information can be introduced into and spread across our networks. I will expand on the measures proposed in the first section below, touching briefly on the non-governmental actors before focusing on what our government can do.

CIVIL SOCIETY—including journalists/investigative journalists and initiatives to track and document Russian influence operations—plays a vital role in both bringing *enhanced clarity about the threat* and *giving Americans defensive tools* via enhanced awareness of Russian information operations and what they aim to achieve; exposing Russian information campaigns and the networks that amplify them; and tracking and illustrating how Russian influence operations work, more broadly. In the future they will also play a vital role in restoring our collective resistance to hostile influence operations. This requires creativity, and resources being directed to civil society initiatives should tolerate some degree of experimentation and failure.

CITIZENS need to be more aware of their information environment. I believe this is a more complicated effort than the promotion of media literacy and fact-checking alone.

INDUSTRY, in particular social media and tech companies, bear a special responsibility in our efforts to respond to Russian information warfare—to remove or contain Russian information architecture from our system. But there are broader questions. After the 2016 election, there was a lot of discussion about Americans 'choosing' to inhabit separate information universes. But what isn't discussed: this is not always a choice, but something being done to us—by targeted advertising, by promoted content, and by algorithms that tell us what we want to see—algorithms that Russian data scientists and information warriors aptly know how to game.

Micro-targeting, hyper-targeting, and individual targeting on social media have one primary application, in a variety of forms: radicalization.There are some uncomfortable questions to be asked here, about whether social media platforms are blindly or knowingly enabling the means for mass psychological operations to radicalize societies and deepen divisions, and whether there are accountability measures required. Facebook in particular has created a means of mass surveillance and collection, and a means of operationalizing information operations effectively and inexpensively—which it acknowledges but downplays.[12] Despite detailed explanations why they bear no legal or moral responsibility for what their engineering has created, Facebook is essentially a real-life, free-market 'big brother'—a platform for surveillance and computational propaganda available to any power willing to pay for it.

The same Russian intelligence-connected company that previously staged a test information assault against the United States—an attack meant to instill fear and mobilize panic[13]—was allowed to buy political advertising targeting Americans during elections.[14] As long as social media platforms refuse to acknowledge the tools and tactics they are enabling, promoting, and profiting from—and explain why they will not take more aggressive steps to protect data privacy, remove revenue possibilities from propagandists, and ensure that content automation isn't gaming algorithms to subvert the minds of human users—then we need to be more aggressive in educating our population about how they are being attacked in the information space and exactly what these attacks aim to achieve. So far, Americans have been offered little clarity of leadership in this regard.

GOVERNMENT plays a vital role in coordinating an effective response to Russian information warfare. This is particularly true in two areas: *political will* and *structural response*. Both are critical, but the importance of political will cannot be undervalued. For example, in Europe, there have been new institutional actors introduced—including the NATO and EU Centres of Excellence, and the EU's East Stratcom Task Force—as well as support given to a range of civil society initiatives—including think tanks like European Values[15]—but the lack of central political will to mount an effective strategy against Russia undercuts these smart initiatives. Our alliance would benefit from American political will galvanizing a *whole-of-alliance approach to securing the information space*.

In the US, I hope political will be in abundance when *enhanced clarity of the threat and its impact* are provided. To counter what is being done to our society by a foreign adversary, we need a *whole-of-government response*. The Russian operational footprint in Europe relies on a core of SVR/FSB/GRU resources, with access to significant technology and information capabilities, operating in a broad lane that asks for creativity and doesn't punish failure,

---

[12] Shane, Scott. "The Fake Americans Russia Created to Influence the Election." *New York Times.* Sept 7, 2017. https://www.nytimes.com/2017/09/07/us/politics/russia-facebook-twitter-election.html   http://www.politico.com/magazine/story/2017/09/08/how-facebook-changed-the-spy-game-215587

[13] Smith, Rohan. "Columbia Chemical hoax tracked to 'troll farm' dubbed the Internet Research Agency." news.-com.au. June 4, 2015. http://www.news.com.au/technology/online/social/columbia-chemical-hoax-tracked-to-trollfarm-dubbed-the-internet-research-agency/news-story/128af54a82b83888158f7430136bcdd1

[14] Shane, Scott & Vindu Goel. "Fake Russian Facebook Accounts Bought $100,000 of Political Ads." *New York Times.* September 6, 2017. https://www.nytimes.com/2017/09/06/technology/facebook-russian-political-ads.html

[15] For European Values' recommendations on how responding to hostile disinformation operations, see: http:// www.europeanvalues.net/wp-content/uploads/2016/06/Full-Scale-Democratic-Response-to-Hostile-Disinformation-Operations-1.pdf

backed by state resources. We have the architecture to be able to build a more effective task force—but we don't. Unity of mission is critical. We need a 'star chamber' coordinating our best assets—diplomatic, military, intelligence, industry, nongovernmental, and informal—to counter the information warfare launched by the Kremlin's 'power vertical.'

Irregular warfare—including information warfare—will need to be fought within our borders. We should define how we do that before the next crisis. To bridge our capabilities gap on an accelerated timeline, we need to review our resources for countering threats in the information space, and we need to *rethink authorities*.

We have forces designed for unconventional warfare: US Army Special Forces. In Europe, for countering Russia, that's the 10th Special Forces Group. This is a group of regionally-aligned, culturally-astute, deep-knowledge forces with the expertise and capabilities to work with local partners to amplify efforts and address critical needs. But practically speaking, they lack the resources, mandate, and technology to act. Instead of giving 10th SFG added resources to *develop a rapid response capability for irregular information warfare*, conduct Military Information Support Operations (MISO), operate in a wider lane in non-conflict countries alongside the State Department in countering these aggressive threats, and coordinate other military and defense assets in this area—this expertise is still in a box. The Marines have recently established a 4-star office dedicated to information operations, led by the Deputy Commandant of Information. There is a whole branch of the Pentagon that specializes in this area. We need this expertise engaged in the fight, and we need to remember that our mil-mil relationships are the steel in the architecture of NATO, which is reinforced by the intelligence backbone of the 'Five Eyes' community.

There is a similar challenge with authorities for US counterintelligence, especially for the FBI and especially in the information space . The Russians have identified a giant[16] blind spot where they can operationalize influence with no interference or oversight (social media). We have to change that equation without falling into the trap of replicating Kremlin tactics.

Clarity on the threat is one of the primary means of *giving Americans defensive tools* against information operations, and engaging them these issues will help *motivate the American populace* and enhance resistance. It is vital to evaluate whether *regulatory measures* can be legislated to enhance data/privacy protections for Americans, limit coercive applications of data driven targeting, and bring transparency to paid content on social media platforms. Again, this is not about limiting the free flow of information and ideas, but restricting the ability for coercive targeting and the simulation of human supporters/movements to promote coercive propaganda.

Finally, government can apply its capabilities in tracking hostile foreign financial flows to *enhance understanding of how Russian money moves in our system*, and what it aims to achieve. President Putin is not some all powerful being. But he has certainty and

---

[16] Rangappa, Asha. "How Facebook Changed the Spy Game." *Politico Magazine*. Sept 8, 2017. http://www.politico.-com/magazine/story/2017/09/08/how-facebook-changed-the-spy-game-215587

seeks to build a cynical world were the only thing that matters is money. That is the 'ideology' the Kremlin exports. And until we understand how that money is poisoning our system of beliefs, he wins.

Our primary failures when it comes to responding to information warfare are failures of imagination, clarity, and coordination. We don't wargame the shadow war. We need to. This is a war we must win.

PREPARED STATEMENT OF MELISSA HOOPER, DIRECTOR OF HUMAN
RIGHTS AND CIVIL SOCIETY PROGRAMS, HUMAN RIGHTS FIRST

Introduction

Senator Gardner, Co-Chair Smith, Ranking Member Cardin, and Members of the Helsinki Commission, I would like to thank you and Chairman Wicker for giving me the opportunity to testify today regarding the damage caused to democracy and human rights globally by Russian disinformation efforts in the United States and in Europe, the efforts of some European countries to respond, and steps the United States should consider to counter Russia's weaponization of information.

I want to address these issues from the perspective of someone who has studied Russia's interference strategies as they operated in Russia during my years living there, and followed their development in Europe, especially after Russia's invasion of Ukraine.

In the United States, we are still grappling with the ramifications of the Russian government's meddling in the 2016 Presidential election. Just last week, Facebook revealed its sale of $100,000 worth of ads promoting divisive social messages to 470 fake, likely-Russian-owned sites. Since the election, Congress and other policy-makers have become increasingly sensitized to the Russian government's use of various forms of disinformation, including Russian-funded media outlets that publish false or misleading stories, automated bots and trolls that disseminate false information to create the appearance of a "grassroots" movement, the use of faux "experts," foundations and think tanks that lend a veneer of credibility to fabricated information, and other methods intended to sow confusion and threaten the foundations of democracy—including the concepts of truth and trust.

The use of disinformation is not the Russian government's sole strategy, but is part of a coordinated effort to disrupt and attack liberal policies, institutions, and norms wherever the opportunity arises, with an overarching goal of fracturing the European Union and the trans-Atlantic alliance. Other strategies include economic influence, in which key figures are offered lucrative deals that implicate them in Russian corruption—such as has occurred in Germany, the UK, and the Czech Republic; electoral disruption, such as funding fringe political parties—as has occurred in Germany and France; and the weakening of multilateral organizations such as the OSCE or UN bodies through obstructionist policies.

At Human Rights First, we have documented the effectiveness of these threats in Eastern Europe, including how Russia has contributed to significant backsliding on democracy and human rights in Poland and Hungary—each a NATO ally. We are seeing Russia make inroads in Central and Eastern Europe through the use of online bots and trolls in Poland, the buying off of politicians and business leaders in Hungary and the Czech Republic, the funding of youth military camps in Hungary and Slovakia, and the dissemination of fabricated stories about migrants and Muslims across Europe, but particularly in Germany.

Contributions to Backsliding in Hungary and Poland; Disruption in Germany

In Hungary, Prime Minister Viktor Orban's government often rubber stamps Kremlin propaganda. The Hungarian government frequently shares the Kremlin's interest in disrupting E.U. policy, unity, and principles of equality and human rights, particularly when it comes to refugee issues. Indeed, the Hungarian government itself often generates false information on migrants, refugees, and the E.U., messages that align with the views of the Kremlin.

Russia has gained a foothold in Hungary through its support for business projects such as the expansion of the PAKS nuclear power plant, the modernization of the Budapest metro, and the MET gas trading enterprise. Russia also funds far-right and paramilitary groups in Hungary.

In Poland, Russophobia runs strong, given the two countries' histories. Today, Russia sponsors around 20 sites that self-identify as "right-wing" Polish websites that do not acknowledge their Russian connections. These outlets work with other disruptive media in Poland to source stories that support the Russian perspective on the E.U., NATO, migrants, and refugees. Russia also disseminates pro-Kremlin propaganda through a network of bots and trolls. In a parallel to our own experience, these programs seek to spread disinformation while making certain ideas appear grassroots-supported.

Importantly, the Hungarian and Polish publics largely disagree with anti-E.U. and anti-democracy messaging. According to several studies, nearly 80% of these populations want to stay in the E.U. and NATO, despite propaganda attacking these institutions. Thus, programs in Eastern Europe that shore up democratic institutions are likely to yield positive returns.

In addition to the propagation of disinformation, Russia also sponsors "Government Organized NGOs," or GONGOs in Poland, Hungary, Germany, and across Europe. These groups, which include advocacy organizations, foundations, and think tanks, put out false or misleading analyses, studies, expert statements, and reports on topics of interest to the Kremlin including on sanctions, Ukraine, migration, E.U. unity, and the efficacy of democracy. Frequently sponsored by oligarchs or organizations with cultural or religious ties to the Kremlin, these GONGOs provide a veneer of legitimacy to misleading data and arguments.

A number of these organizations espouse the neo-Eurasianist philosophy of Kremlin advisor Alexander Dugin, who argues that democracy is waning globally. We now see Eurasian think tanks and NGOs cropping up all over Europe, including via websites that actively traffic in false information. Two pro-Kremlin Eurasian organizations are particularly active putting out information ahead of the upcoming election in Germany. The German Center for Eurasian Studies is based in Berlin. The other—the European Center for Geopolitical Analysis—is based in Warsaw.

A clear example of how the Kremlin has employed disinformation in conjunction with other strategies of disruption is its use of false stories about migrants, refugees, and Muslims, and the threats they allegedly present to national security and public health. In partnership with far-right parties in Germany, the Kremlin has weaponized these false stories to sow fear and distrust, a wedge that it uses to undercut support for Angela Merkel and the CDU.

As a number of studies have shown, our brains are wired to increasingly believe a statement is true the more often we hear it. Russia has become expert at using this brain science against us, carefully repeating false facts—in this instance, about Muslim immigrants.

At Human Rights First, we call the spread of social media targeting minority communities, abetted by disinformation, "weaponized speech." Next month we'll be issuing a report on how to combat it.

One well-known example of weaponized speech is the 2016 so-called "Lisa F. case." It is the story of a 13-year old Russian-German girl in Germany who didn't come home one night. Russian media spread a false narrative that she was kidnapped and raped by Muslim migrants.

German police debunked this story soon after interviewing the alleged victim. Yet Russian media, German far-right parties, and Russian political leaders (including Foreign Minister Sergei Lavrov), continued to promulgate the false story. These voices urged the Russlanddeutsche, ethnic Germans who lived for generations in Russia but have now returned to Germany, to question whether the German police were covering up the alleged crimes of migrants for political reasons.

As a result, thousands of Russlanddeutsche came out into German streets to protest the alleged cover-up and Angela Merkel's migration policy. Protests concerning a non-event are the stuff of dreams for the Kremlin, as they cause Europeans to question their institutions and their values of democracy and tolerance.

The German Election: Russian-funded Think Tanks and German Far-Right Parties

I conducted my own research into Russian disinformation in Germany earlier this year. I was interested in Russia's use of think tanks, particularly in the run-up to Germany's September election, and their possible link to the far-right and ultra-nationalist parties Alternative fur Deutschland (AfD) and National Democratic Party (NPD).

I knew that AfD's top candidate on the party slate, Alexander Gauland, had traveled to Russia last year and met with Alexander Dugin. He also met the head of a Berlin-based Russian think tank, Boris Yakunin. AfD has also possibly received funding from the Kremlin. I also knew that leaders of the neo-Nazi NPD had attended a conference in St. Petersburg at the invitation of Russian Deputy Prime Minister Dmitry Rogozin, and that NPD had publicly expressed support for Putin and pro-Russian policies in Germany.

I tracked the information, statements, and papers put out by two Berlin-based, Russian-funded organizations: the Dialogue of Civilizations—Yakunin's organization, and the Center for Continental Cooperation, now called the German Center for Eurasian Studies. I also tracked the statements and policy papers of AfD and NPD leaders.

What I found was that the Russian-funded think tanks and German far-right parties were putting out similar messages on a number of key topics including the E.U., NATO, the United States, Western democracy, and Western media. In general, these included attacks on multilateral institutions built on liberal democratic values, and indictments of these institutions as serving only elites. Specifically, both argued that Western democracy had been degraded by multiculturalism, that Western media was untrustworthy, that the E.U. and the U.S. were not truly free or democratic, and that the U.S. used NATO and other tools to subject the world to its hegemony.

It bears noting that the reach of these campaigns is at present quite small. Overall, Germany seems to be prepared to fend off interference around its upcoming election. Learning from the experiences of the recent U.S. and French elections, German leaders have issued public warnings about potential Russian cyberattacks and disinformation. The German public has therefore been sensitized to the possibility of interference.

However, success is not a foregone conclusion. About three million Russian speakers are being targeted daily with disinformation about refugees, same-sex marriage, terrorism, and defense issues. Merkel's pro-U.S. stance, and support for liberal democratic values, is being used by Russia to exploit anti-Americanism and anti-migrant sentiment.

Germany has also made some missteps in responding to disinformation. The Network Enforcement Act it passed in June essentially forces social media companies to be the arbiter of what constitutes free speech and what violates German law. This is a dangerous, short-sighted approach that will inevitably force corporations to rely heavily on censorship. The danger of this approach can be seen in the fact that Russia saw fit to pass an almost identical version of the German law. Ukraine is also dangerously responding with a wave of censorship.

The patterns I have described are by now familiar because we have seen them here at home: Russia's disinformation campaigns discredit democratic institutions, such as elections and independent media, and are accompanied by other strategies of interference, such as the use of corruption to infiltrate policy-making bodies, the employment of faux experts to echo Russia's false claims, and the funding of disruptive agents such as extreme political parties and movements.

We need to act comprehensively against these strategies.

In January, then-Director of National Intelligence James Clapper said that the attacks that occurred around the U.S. presidential election were a "clarion call" for action "against a threat to the very foundation of our democratic political system." This threat is not confined to the immediate run-up to elections. Foreign challenges to our democracy are occurring right now, and the U.S. has so far been slow to respond.

How the U.S. Can Combat Russian Disinformation

So, what do we do?

First, the U.S. government needs to unify around the conviction that Russia uses disinformation in the United States. By no means is it the only purveyor of false and misleading information here, but it remains a leader in pursuing this phenomenon for political ends. The U.S. government needs to present a united front to European allies in combating this threat, and take a leadership role in crafting a thorough and methodical response. The current presidential administration has not provided leadership in this regard. Congress should thus remind our European allies that the U.S. stands strong in its values, and is ready to partner with them to fight interference by foreign powers that seek to undermine democracy.

Second, Congress needs to work with other government bodies, tech companies, and civil society to gain a more comprehensive understanding of how disinformation works and can be combatted—and shouldn't rely on short-sighted responses similar to the German law and the censorship it incentivizes.

A thoughtful approach to online disinformation will involve: (1) combating the use of bots that robotically amplify information and articles based on programmed algorithms, given that the U.S. does not protect the free speech of computer programs; (2) working with experts in civil society to examine laws around online speech to ensure they are informed not only by the first amendment, but also by the experiences of affected communities; and (3) creating an appeals process whereby consumers can contest instances of content removal, and receive quick and efficient redress.

Third, while much of the U.S. government's focus has been on messaging and public diplomacy, we also need long-term strategies to support democratic institutions and values overseas. Last year, Senators Portman and Murphy passed legislation that allotted $80 million to the State Department's Global Engagement Center for programs to combat disinformation, including Russian disinformation. Secretary Tillerson has approved the use of $60 million of these funds by the State Department to combat disinformation put out by terrorist groups such as the Islamic State. This funding is important. At the same time, however, we need to recognize that putting out better messaging about what democratic institutions can accomplish, or responding to specific false messaging campaigns, is an incomplete response. Doing so is like treating the symptoms of an illness, rather than curing the disease. The best advertisement for democracy and human rights is the demonstration of strong, well-functioning democratic institutions—not just more messages about what these institutions could be. We need to show people, not just tell them.

On the part of Congress, this means adequately funding democracy and governance programming, including in Eastern Europe, a region that we formerly thought had "graduated" from authoritarianism.

One strategy that Congress should support is the European and Eurasian Democracy and Anti-Corruption Initiative, which was introduced by a bipartisan coalition, including some on this Commission. This legislation would commit $157 million for innovative projects to combat Russian disinformation and influence in Europe. Indeed, the Senate's current State and Foreign Operations bill contains $120 million for Countering Russian Influence.

With these funds, the Department of State could support regional programs to bolster democracy and human rights, including in countries where the U.S. does not currently have a USAID office, such as Poland and Hungary. The funds could support media literacy, like what we believe is helping Germany fend off Russian influence this election, and support independent media to counter Russian disinformation. These programs can increase the critical eye of media consumers. They should also support local civic leaders to hold governments accountable when they engage in corruption, threaten the rule of law, or flout the basic values and requirements of E.U. and NATO membership—actions which show the strength of democratic principles.

Conclusion

At a time in which democratic values and institutions are being undermined and challenged directly by Russia through a concerted, multifaceted effort, we need to invest resources in these mainstays of sustainable security and prosperity. Now more than ever, the United States needs to maintain the leadership role we have held since the last World War in supporting democratic norms and values. Nations the world over are looking to us for guidance in dealing with this new type of threat to our institutions and ideals. We need to step up.

Thank you.

○

This is an official publication of the
**Commission on Security and
Cooperation in Europe.**

This publication is intended to document
developments and trends in participating
States of the Organization for Security
and Cooperation in Europe (OSCE).

All Commission publications may be freely
reproduced, in any form, with appropriate
credit. The Commission encourages
the widest possible dissemination
of its publications.

http://www.csce.gov   @HelsinkiComm

The Commission's Web site provides
access to the latest press releases
and reports, as well as hearings and
briefings. Using the Commission's electronic
subscription service, readers are able
to receive press releases, articles,
and other materials by topic or countries
of particular interest.

Please subscribe today.

www.ingramcontent.com/pod-product-compliance
Lightning Source LLC
Chambersburg PA
CBHW081317250726
48662CB00008B/2625